sightlines

ESSENTIAL POETS SERIES 239

Canada Council   Conseil des Arts
for the Arts   du Canada

ONTARIO ARTS COUNCIL
CONSEIL DES ARTS DE L'ONTARIO

an Ontario government agency
un organisme du gouvernement de l'Ontario

Canada

Guernica Editions Inc. acknowledges the support of the Canada Council
for the Arts and the Ontario Arts Council. The Ontario Arts Council
is an agency of the Government of Ontario.

We acknowledge the financial support of the Government of Canada.
Nous reconnaissons l'appui financier du gouvernement du Canada.

sightlines

Henry Beissel

GUERNICA
EDITIONS
TORONTO • BUFFALO • LANCASTER (U.K.)
2016

Michael Mirolla, general editor
Cover and interior design, David Moratto
Front cover art, Arlette Francière
Author photo, Clara Boisvert
Guernica Editions Inc.
1569 Heritage Way, Oakville, (ON), Canada L6M 2Z7
2250 Military Road, Tonawanda, N.Y. 14150-6000 U.S.A.
www.guernicaeditions.com

Distributors:
University of Toronto Press Distribution,
5201 Dufferin Street, Toronto (ON), Canada M3H 5T8
Gazelle Book Services, White Cross Mills, High Town, Lancaster LA1 4XS U.K.

First edition.
Printed in Canada

Legal Deposit—First Quarter
Library of Congress Catalog Card Number: 2015952397
Library and Archives Canada Cataloguing in Publication
Beissel, Henry, 1929-, author
Sightlines / Henry Beissel. -- 1st edition.
(Essential poets series ; 239)
Poems.
Issued in print and electronic formats.
ISBN 978-1-77183-132-1 (paperback).--ISBN 978-1-77183-133-8
(epub).--ISBN 978-1-77183-134-5 (mobi)

I. Title. II. Series: Essential poets series ; 239

PS8503.E39S55 2016   C811'.54   C2015-906651-4   C2015-906652-2

sightlines

Contents

1. so many worlds to see ...

2. away from home ...

3. time weighing in the bones ...

1. so many worlds to see ...

Through the Rain's Eyes

I've watched the news and walk down the lane
into the forest where the rain's voice is still green
as August. The trees lean into the light like crows,
their trunks black and glossy; their branches follow
the crooked ways of the wind that delivers autumn,
willy-nilly, with a cold eye. No bird sings in this
weather. Leaves, wet and still green, fall to the ground,
numb and mute, one by one—
                              like famished children
along a dusty track in Somalia or in Sudan: suddenly
something gives, the force that holds the parts in place
lets go ... Except that the desert speaks in tongues
of fire, sucks bodies dry till they drop, emaciated,
dying in the crooked ways of a world of plenty.

Wet leaves begin to mat the forest floor between
wild garlic, wild mushrooms and wintergreen.
They stick to the soles of my boots and cluster
until I walk on lily-pads as though to polish
the many mirrors the rain has cast across my path,
pools reflecting larger worlds in miniature reflecting
worlds to be seen clearly through the rain's eyes.

You cannot count the leaves in this patch of forest,
or at night the stars in this patch of sky, no more than the tears
shed in Somalia or in the slums of Bombay, Bogota,
Brazzaville—continents of sick and hungry children—
you can count them one by one every 22 seconds, makes
35,000 per day, totalling 12,775,000 dying every year.
Can you measure their pain? Or their mothers' grief?

A spider has hung a row of raindrops out to dry
between ferns, trapping in each a world where
everything is upside down: trees dance on clouds,
the rain jets up in countless sputtering fountains,
and I hang by my feet from a patch of earth lost
in a wobbling globe. The wind bends and stretches
the trees, bends and stretches my legs, then plucks me off
the line, drops me ...
                          I fall headfirst, spatter on the ground
and lie shattered among fragments of forest and sky.
Thus images shatter in the rain's eyes just like the credulous
images that shatter in the breaking eyes of children—
kaleidoscopes of what might have been. Hunger plucks them
from their life-lines, drops and buries them without ceremony
in the ever drifting sands of all the saharas of our madness.

The rain washes the trees, washes my face,
but it cannot wash the stain from my heart.
The wet leaves on the trees shudder in the wind,
the dampness draws the cold to my skin; I shiver.
September brings home a promise of new seasons,
but the children of Somalia shall never hear
what the still green voice of the rain whispers.

The rain's eyes have sightlines that conceal
nothing. They embrace a drama whose plot
is contrived by grasping hands and unfolds
against the backdrop of this careless forest.
Learn the lines for your bit part as you walk back
to the house. Intermission is almost over, and we're all
on stage for the final act that'll run far into the night.

Ayorama

(for Arlette)

1.

I've walked many seasons the crooked path
I cut and carved through this Glengarry wilderness
following the turns of boulders and the twists
of tree trunks to clear a lane wide enough for two
to ponder the absurdity of being there. We
cannot flit like chipmunks between ferns
and goldenrod, nor swing from tree to tree
like our distant cousins — we must have level
ground to bend the mind to broken planes.

Not a straight line in sight, said the Scot
who drove the dozer. *I aim to keep it that way,*
I avowed and told him to turn south by the hard
maple then west behind the butternut south again
around the basswood follow the bull moose
tracks east to the sitting-bear rock after that
go north northwest by the oak ... *Crazy as a coon,*
he muttered under the raucous breath of his
diesel engine, but shouted *You're the boss!*
thinking truly his machine was, revving it up to roar
and pounce with iron paw, push aside petrified
aeons and gouge out an eccentric circle back
to the loghouse where the trail begins and ends.

I too have had to brutalize the silence I came
to recover. How else could the forest have taken me
into its arms and I have embraced it had I not
stepped close enough to feel smell taste
its body, close enough for us to enter each other?
Even diminished as you are by the cruellest
animal to stalk this planet and conquer it,
your presence still overwhelms my senses
with a ceremony of communion, a ritual of
transfiguration more ancient than memory.

2.

Prehistoric glaciers and earthquakes, continental
shifts and collisions, stellar bombardment,
millennia of rainstorms heatwaves blizzards
laid out this landspace without forethought,
raised tall as a hawk's steep fall red pine and white
spruce, black oak and yellow birch, to take
under their green stalwart wings rabbit and racoon,
at random, bear and beaver, white-tailed deer
and beady squirrel, skunk, fox and coyote. Lofty
spaces woven of tangled shadows on thin spindles
of slanting light where grouse screech owl bluejay
oriole cardinal and warbler nest between song
and silence under a sky that reaches forever
and ever wordless beyond measure into unknowing.
Homeless as humans we made our home there.

Before I gathered these timbers
time had worn away all
that was extraneous already.
The space they sheltered for a century
and more had been abandoned.
They watched the infants
flushed from womb water into air
scream at the light, struggle
to come to terms with the lot
they had not chosen, and return
to the dust and darkness
whence they had emerged
into the twilight of a settler's cabin.

Spring was a bursting of seed and sod.
The logs held the seasons in place
bridling the heat of summers
bent on horses and hay, corn and cattle.
Kept the autumnal rains to their promise
of feeding creek and pond. Stood up
to winter howling at the door,
rattling windows, battering the cabin
with ice fists in snow gloves.

Survivors too must die.
The same weathers that wiped their lives
off the now forgotten stones
tilting at weeds in gardens of memory
left their homesteads empty shells
scattered across Glengarry. Rainstorms
and blizzards gnawed away the shingled
roofs, leaving the rafters a ribcage
of the beast that devoured them.
Carcasses of farms that struggled
with drought, debt and depression
in vain. Now skunks and squirrels
nest in the mouldering silences between
jumbled tin and timber. Graveyard
of pioneer dreams and aspirations.

Till I brought these cedar logs north
four concessions and reassembled them,
hewed, heaved and fitted them
for a new lease on life and love.
Soon they were at home among spruce
maples cedars aspen ash birch and
joisted and raftered they became home
to us. Did some residue of the voices
and labours of generations long buried
still linger between phloem and pith
in the heartwood to bear witness
to what the bones always know
even while the flesh dreams?

3.

Ayorama is a love story. I have never been alone
here. You, my love, came early to join me
in these backwoods lost between two cities.
The logs were barely bound to each other
and the ramshackle floors expected pioneers,
not high heels. Blackflies and mosquitoes
held sway that spring across the untamed woods,
but the nights and the summer were ours.

For more than three decades Orion visited
our sleep with his star-spangled sword, Jupiter
and Mars wandered up and down the shingled
roof while sun and moon painted fleeting
patterns across the pond. I worked the world's
iniquities into the soil and in their time and place
light and water, fire and air conspired to raise
a green harvest sufficient to feed a multitude.
At dawn the nights yielded what sustains a garden
in the mind. In the twilight came the shape of words.

4.

Passion powers a process that carries us beyond
ourselves to engender beauty precisely
at the comical moment when flesh and flower
want a voice to be heard speaking from the podium
at the centre of their tempestuous tranquillity.

You raised your belly naked to the August sun
and on a skyblue morning the primal sea broke
into your solitude and by nightfall a child was born
to us in defiance of the probabilities of fate. She
grew here from egg and sperm to womanhood
instructed by a harsh taskmaster in the school
of flora and fauna that eloquently teach verities
of innocence and experience blunt as winter
and spring between tree-house and ice-wind lane.

Such flowering of flesh into mind hallows the forest,
its spaces domed under vaults branches construct
fanning arches from the trees' pillars against the sky,
the footpath an aisle between anguish and chance.

5.

There is no way to redress the injuries axes
and chainsaws inflict on birches and cedars,
oaks and beeches, though I have tried. Profit
is the world's executioner. Cats and dozers
erase forests, steel traps eliminate wolf and beaver,
rifles exterminate bear and moose. We poison
and plunder all habitats as if we owned them,
though I never cast net or bait in the lake
I had dug and seeded with fish—the long-legged heron
took care of that: elegantly, aloof as a connoisseur,
with chopsticks sharp as a spear he picked them
from the water in languid flight, like choice morsels
one at a time, and swallowed them whole.

We knew love's labour alone can turn wilderness
into a garden; but we learnt that it must yet remain
wilderness. You elaborated your instincts to nurture
and protect with acts of beauty as I struggled to create
a balance between the imperatives of nature and art,
leaving the long and the short of it to their discretion.

Slowly acid rain trained moss to cover fifty loads
of gravel on the poet-philosopher's path
I walked time and again till I understood from
the soles of my feet up this neck of the woods
owns me. Soft knowledge that finds peace
in surrender. Wherever I go, Ayorama
will raise my bones tantalizing to the sky.

6.

How to bid thee farewell when you cannot hear
even your own voices? The wind haranguing
ash pine and tamarack each in a different tongue,
the sap singing the seasons' melodies under the bark,
the medley of sounds ten thousand creatures make
to command and maintain their place in the sun—
what words can make this parting memorable?

I learnt to read the aspen trembling at the edge
of a storm, the cardinal's punctuated whistle
who pecked at his own image in the glass
when I whistled back from my den three short sharp
glissandos down to a rapid-fire shrill, the outraged
shrieks of bluejays determined to drive me away
from nests I never saw, the spit and hiss of squirrels
and wild geese, the jumpy deer in the orchard,
the circling hawk—who will I be without them?

The smell of pine in the spring air, a taste of mint
on summer's tongue, the maple flames, a raspberry's
velvet touch and the crunch of snow and ice
under fur boots drew me into the season's dance
spinning everlasting death into the delirium of living.

7.

Ayorama hung the planet in my study like a *perpetuum
mobile* suspended from the sky. How else could I
have recovered the music my father played me
in the cradle? Melodies lost in the jangle of terror
and tyranny till I heard them again in the bullfrogs'
bassoons, the soprano voices of birds, the pizzicato
chipmunks, an owl's misty call, the whispering wind,
a hush of snow, the dark hum of summer? How else
could I have recovered that lost child and moved
atonal meaning through music into mute assent?

You made it possible for me to put down the burdens
of this bloodshot age, lean them against your trees
while I searched day and night for the well and web
of understanding. Never were the stars more loud and clear
in pointing the way from one darkness to another.

That's how I found a voice and my love the images
that will speak to us long after we have moved
to other spaces, other sounds. The deer harvested
the apples in the orchard, ample every other year,
picked them from the branches on their hindlegs
or dug them up from under the snow. The fruit
that ripened in the orchard of the imagination
must feed us now in the urban years to come, even if
we have to dig it up from under the ice of a winter
of the mind. It too provides a harvest ample enough
to share with all who still know how to look and listen.

8.

The girl who saw the deer and heard the voices
of the forest has spread her wings and flown the nest.
Every fawn learns to dare the future's promise.
Then is the time too for the parents to move on—
time for us to move into the city as we move
into winter. Already flocks of wild geese surprise
the evening with the shrill lament of their departure.
Feathered arrows across a bloodied sun. Flight
into an uncertain future. Soon the fir trees will fold
their wings under the pressure of snow. Ash and poplar
stand unleaved in the naked cold that will test our mettle.
But in the midst of winter it was fire put us to the test
—the ultimate test of endurance and renewal.

9.

We built Ayorama not for eternity
but for generations to come,
sat around the fieldstone fireplace
to share with friends alive and dead
the joy and the burden of knowing
the short, ample measure of things,
raised a child there, engendered
others, less tangible and therefore,
perhaps, more durable — word
creatures and painterly beings —
all in search and celebration
of the incomprehensible world
that gives us light so that we can see
the darkness.

            Past midnight, at the hour
when arsonists prowl the impotence
of their blistering brains, fire broke out
at the east end of the house. No one saw
the prowler, no one was at home.
The flames raced along the desiccated
timbers, bit through the shingled roof
and screamed at the sky. Freezing rain came
down, too slow and too thin to match
the fury of the fire. Windows exploded,
beams became torches. No one came
and no one could have come in time
to put out the flames lit in foul play.

10.

Not all who listen hear.
Shall I speak of the neighbour
willing to kill for a foot
of land he imagines part
of his ill-begotten lot?
A good fence will not
make him a better man.
He is deaf to the wild
and its creatures, to the make
believe stars that puncture
all boasts and leave him
more silly than his tail
wagging dog when he barks.

Or shall I speak of the stranger
with the mango-mellowed
tongue that talks seeming
into being? A limp handshake
seals a sly purchase.

Not all who look see.
Shall I tear the mask
of peace and piety
off the arcadian idyll
of rural living? Not
all that's picturesque
is also salubrious,
even in the unpolluted
air of the woods.

Better to remember
the neighbours who learnt
the give and take of labour
and harvest, seasons, sickness,
youth and old age. Hewing
wood and milking cows,
they know we are in transit
here, guests at the mercy
of a world at once
hospitable and hostile,
where the clouds are our neighbours
and the groundhogs burrowing
under the fence we must love
each other or perish.

11.

The police arrived to witness a blazing
pyre, summoned us from unimpeachable sleep
lest someone was trapped inside: they
did not report the tales of lives lived and loved
from the heights of happiness to the pits
of pain and sorrow, did not see the labour of decades
burning prematurely to cinders. Dawn saw
only a blackened chimney towering. Tombstone
for a history too brief for time's annals. A pile
of fallen timbers, charred and glazed
with a thin crust of ice even as fire crept still
crackling through the logs' heartwood. Soon
racoons and chipmunks will clamber all over
the rubble, and rats may find a home here.

12.

What will the lessons of a hundred acres avail us where
monsters of steel, glass and cement have devoured
the forests and their inhabitants whose lives we shared
for three decades? Pride and ambition have choked
the breath out of this land with streets and alleys
crowded with imperial creatures puffed with the power
of hundreds of horses, noisy creatures with venomous
breath, robots surpassing Ayorama's creatures
in everything except curiosity, affection and fear.
Cities have given birth to beauty unknown to birds
or trees, but must they pay for it with their lives?

13.

I must learn again to abide the whistle of authority,
the hiss and spit of the hucksters of news and wares,
the posturing of con-artists honoured for what is trite
and truthless as they humbug their way to tawdry fame
and the applause and admiration of what is worthless
by the gullible multitude. In the silence of a star-blazed night
in the company of pines and birches, foxes and grouse,
you can forget all that comes with membership
in this species mutated from rats, scurrying to and fro
between slot-machines and combustion engines right up
on their hindlegs but not upright in the search
for their lost selves, you forget you belong to a species
bug-eyed for instant gratification, chasing its own tail
as though it were the holy grail. We know not who we are
or where we're going. Greed springs a leak in the mind
and leaves a vacuum, and the jackpot turns out to be
empty when the chips are down. By hook and by crook
you cannot harvest happiness or fetch fulfilment.
Only fools think hype and chutzpah are life forces.
Give me the soft touch of a lady's slipper in flower.

14.

You, my love, wanted the city
and must now be my companion
in the search for new beginnings.
The intricate play of light and shade
across Glengarry fields and forests
hovers around us like the ghosts
of a sensual affair come to a bad end.
Dance of fireflies in the noisier nights
as dusk falls across the memory.

15.

In the urban hustle
and among strangers
to weave a new web
of adventure and affirmation
and yet remain true.

I shall plug my ears and listen
to the voices speaking inside me
straight from Ayorama's mouth.
They tell me the blue heron
carries the universe on his wings
and the artful lupines
have colourcoded its secrets.

In the city too there are trees
and where there are trees
there are robins to deliver dawn.
I shall converse with those
who see when they look
and hear when they listen.
I'll laugh with them
knowing tomorrow
is no more probable
than today was yesterday.

16.

A tree uprooted
may yet extend its being
from darkness to light.
But light is fire:
it lives and dies by consuming
what it fetches from darkness.

17.

Ayorama is no more
than a time and place
in the mind now.
Without a tongue
the wind has nothing
to tell us except
that it blows
blows forever
and deposits our voices
in the fields and forests
of eternal silence.

A Poet's Path Revisited

Seven years gone and the path still winds its way
        languidly through the wilderness
of my dreams, starting where imagination
        brushed lines, shapes, colours
into landscapes of the mind responding to nature's
        prompts where the heron poises
still as a stone statue to snatch fish and frog from the edge
        of the pond whose waters rise still
from the molten remains of ancient bygone glaciers.

The path skirts the artist's studio, then plunges
        southwest into the woods
where he used to pause on his walks to listen
        to the aspen whisper on the wind
before entering the green tunnel between cedars
        pines, sumac, and wild apple trees
planted at random by the digestive grace
        of squirrels, grouse and deer
plus the bluster of the heady air too easily
        troubled by any passing weather.

Past the venerable butternut whose bark is grooved
   like an unruly surf frozen in midair
the path now turns east to where a soaring ash
   has hoisted a tree-house straight up
on limbless trunk into the sky, too high to climb
   except on Jacob's ladder.
But the hunters knew nothing of angels in their blind
   as they waited for an antlered stag
to wander incautiously into the cross-hair of their gun
   and fired to kill the beast with the beauty.

The path curves now through the sepia spaces
   of an open sugar-bush, meanders
between ferns and blackberry bushes and points
   north, my love, to the pole star
around which we spin ceaselessly at 1,000 km/h
   to emerge at the other edge of the pond
across from the loghouse that completed the circle
   in a raging fire a few steps
from where the path ends at the door of a lowly hut
   that sheltered a poet's multiverse.

There, in the den of my dreams, worlds were born
   with the flick of a pen, war and peace
shook the earth and rent the skies at the mercy of language:
   what might be and what is clashed
as words confronted what they tried to say—rhythm and image
   offered coordinates to locate experience
and call the incomprehensible to order. Turning and turning
   with the spin of planets and particles
I awake on the path thinking cuts across the bewildering landscape
   of mind and matter, and walk on.

But the latitudes and longitudes of language stay in place,
   providing maps to the matter of my dreams
and guidance to the search for treasures buried in the mind
   for a future archaeologist to mine.

Ash Tree Greening

(for Clara)

Summer is the trees' season
though the ash is slow getting there,
slow coming out of its winter coma,
stretching green fingers towards the sun
inch by inch till they have raised a dome
of shade the birds want to inhabit.
Nuthatch grosbeaks finches jays —
they move in late to chase and chatter
where a feeder hangs that saw the stalwart
through the bleak months of ice and snow:
they're at home here now more than I am.

A green summer wind turns the ash
into a shimmering sphere struggling
to break free from its anchor deep
in the earth. Its interior remains calm
harbouring its own memories, of storms
and frost or the woodpeckers' shocking
visits, but also of children and lovers,
of those whose gaze it can raise to the sky.

Remnants of a tree house—a few planks
rotting askew in its branches remember
a child's games that turned many a summer
into dreams of freedom as girl became woman.
I never saw lovers loving in its shade
though in the heat of August the ash tree
invites such pleasures without shame,
offering to shelter their tenderness
against the torrid light running off
its leaves like torrents of green rain.

In fall the ash tree clings to its leaves
till the green is drained from them;
they return to the colour of earth
and rough cold-fingered winds pluck them
one by one, crumpling them on the ground.
This is when I climbed its peak, hoisting
myself up the ladder its branches held out,
invading a privacy of birds to put
my pluck to the test and reach the top
where hawk and raven perch. I sat there
pressed against the trunk, the bark
furrowing my back stiff and green with fear
and surveyed the dizzy woods: so many
worlds to visit travelling by tree.

Soon the ash will withdraw its offers
and retire into winter solitude,
standing naked when it most needs cover,
its stamina fed from roots that know
the greening of more springs and summers
than children and lovers can muster.

Leap into the Light

(for my grandson Bennett)

The pulse that pumped the seed prompted
the drumbeat that woke you—a soft nimble

pounding to summon generations for an assembly
of parts to embody an ancient blueprint.

The blind seed found its partner and blindly
they embraced the intricate symmetries

where to draw the strength and hone the skills
for a bold leap breaching the surface of darkness.

You are that leap into the light. Newborn
you burst in a flurry of promise and potential

from histories recorded in star tracks and stone
to protest life stridently against oblivion.

Who knows what shudder at the cosmic birth
sent light years eddying across the void

to spin electrons around protons into vortexes
that still ignite millions of suns each day.

They catch fire in the centrifuge of galaxies
and spread energy to animate dead matter.

You'll learn to walk upright into that mystery
on a planet that's but a hiccup in a cloud of dust.

We are composed of what rain washed from rock
and the inexorable wind carried across land and sea—

fruit of fusion and diffusion at play in a patch of light
passing between one impenetrable darkness and another.

Yet in that leap and play lies the key to all the wonders
of the world that whet your appetite for living.

Playful, we poke the membrane of what appears to be
real, groping for the tempting how and the enigmatic why

in things and their shadows, push open doors, windows
of perception, inch by inch, until our senses are wide

awake and clamour to rejoice in the passion of being
here and there being an infinite recession of reasons.

Today's seas are turbulent and the coming storms
will exact a price for overdrawing our allotment.

The tempests of our passion have driven us off-course.
Tomorrow is your chance to pilot the ship home.

It's a stormy, unforgiving sea you'll have to cross
in a ship whose engines are failing, whose crew is waking

from a dream of lotusland too late to find their bearings,
and a killer wind is tearing the sails we hoist to shreds.

Lunacy is already the order of the day. The captain
is counting gold coins in his cabin while desperate

passengers brawl between decks to reach derelict lifeboats
monster waves will capsize before they are launched.

Such is the winter of the age you are born into
with the promise of another spring and the power

to blossom and translate anguish into music and dance
that are the mind's own purpose and fulfillment.

Let not the pain of living consciously diminish its joys.
The seasons wheel all things through the phases

of the moon and the conflagrations of the sun. Watch
a spring dawn hang dewdrops out to dry in a spider's

web while the early light sings with the voices of birds
and flowers break into exclamations of colour.

Feel a soft summer wind fondle you velvet and
fragrant in the arms of your first eternal love.

Smell the heavy bouquet of an autumn afternoon,
rich with decay and renewal, its light maturing

to a glass of sherry as you toast the anniversary
of trees at their carnival of heedless dancing leaves.

Taste the first snowflake and know winter
is a sleigh ride from the top of your dreams

to the depths of your delight in defiance down
the long slope of never ending merry-go-round

stories that tell the wind all your adventures, all
your moments of ecstasy in which beauty turns

into truth before silence returns to the forests
you explored, the seas you sailed, the cities you built.

Life is a mixed bag bursting at the seams with trivia
and surprises. Between the week's science and lit classes,

Saturday's soccer game and Sunday's concert there are
worlds of beauty, corruption and mystery to explore.

Between mom's chicken soup and your predilection
for desserts there is enough food for thought to tantalize

your insatiable curiosity for a dozen lifetimes. Against
the daily grind I recommend exercises in bravado.

One needs to grow wings and fly beyond the petty turmoil
born of ambition, greed and ignorance. But remember

Icarus. The moth's craving for the candle is stilled once
only, yet we must reach forever for what we cannot grasp.

Supreme ecstasy springs from knowing freedom
and to be free we must learn to unknow everything

we know so that we can become what we are: part
of the whole where Phoenix soars into another dawn.

Camping Out

It's as though the crimson sun
before slipping over the horizon
had put its finger to earth's lips
to sanctify this hour with silence.

One by one the stars light up
the night's raven-feathered dome
that shelters all our fearful stores
of love and longing forever.

All day long the rains beat
the storm's drums on our tent
and howling winds danced around us
like a band of frenzied flagellants.

They lashed the lake, cutting deep
welts across the water and whipping
waves into an incongruous surf
ragged as the rocky shore.

And we ran naked between trees
that were whirlpools of leaves.
Knotted rainthongs lashed us into ecstasy
till we outshouted the thunder in the clouds.

No one heard us, no one could
hear us. The birds saw the storm come
and took shelter, leaving us to our high-
flying selves in the spiked wind.

Oh for that fleeting barefoot encounter
with eternity when the toes are intimate
with heather and grass, and the skin tastes
primeval oceans! Then is oneness without name.

The damp cold brought us back down
as a heavy grey curtain rose to reveal
the bloodied sun like a rubiate pearl
coming to rest in the hand of darkness.

Now the woods are closing in on us.
Night is on the prowl, stings, claws and fangs
at the ready. Danger drips from wet leaves.
We huddle close in the shivering gloom.

We're meant to be at home here, my love,
in this wilderness. But a tent doesn't deter
a hungry bear. A thin moon floats on the lake
—a silver canoe from one darkness to another.

Night Reflections

It's one of the small hours
when the aged die in their sleep
while infants cry out
for consolation at their mother's breast.
Those on shift now get to feel
the weight of time in every bone.

What woke me,
what drew me to the window?
A face limned dark on dark,
its features washed out
like the weathered sculpture
on an ancient tombstone.
It hangs in midair,
an eerie sketch on glass.

The night is hot
and soundless the fireflies
set off their tiny charges of light.
I catch the glint
of many knives beyond
the circle of darkness.
A throat. A wrist.
Cut. Is it the pain
that woke me and
now withholds sleep?

Recognition always comes
as a shock. A sleight of the eye
has cast the face in the glass
out among the trees
like some ghost of the woods—
my face, pale,
more mask than portrait,
the eyes holes gaping
as black as the flowers
out in the garden,
shafts deep down
where they mine
the ore of nightmares.
I hang there
in the spruce tree
suspended from shadows
hearing in the void
sighs, laughter, screams.

By the pond a bullfrog
throbs *basso profondo*.
Lovers have long drifted off
into their post-coital utopias.
The stars are not
where they claim to be.

My face is
impaled on the spruce tree's
spiked branches
where thin and chilly
a faint glitter
etches shadows
under my eyes.

The sky strains
asteroids and meteors,
galaxies and supernovae
from the distant light
and then disperses them
in the dark grey of trees.

I cannot see the trails
a myriad creatures leave
who crowd the dark
with a life richer
than my audio-visual world.
I see only the brooding
night reflections on the glass.

Group of Seven Trees

1. Fred Varley's Cedars

Arms curved as tenderly as birds' wings
they dance with all the grace and poise
of ballerinas, wilder and more sensuous,
along the edge of the plateau where
the mountain peaks can watch them
huddled in purple silence.
                         Everything is
alive here: you can feel the branches sway
with relief that they are free still of winter's
burden of snow that has already limned
the distant Seymour Range, you can smell
the aromatic wood, hear the waxwings chatter
in the shade and the creek down below
ripple over rocks.
                  The cedars are dancing
on a breeze, dancing a late summer ballet
draped in veils dappled in many greens
and browns that flow like the bow waves
of a river boat as though the mountains
and the valley were churning two seasons
into one journey into the blue grey sky.

Music choreographs the colours on this canvas
to dance the rites of summer riotous into fall.

2. A.Y. Jackson's Maples

Stems no thicker than a finger the maples
bend their youthful limbs over the creek
swaying, nodding in the wind perhaps to invite
a veery to survey the rapids. A flock of crimson
butterflies clings to them—leaves too young
to die though some are already floating
downstream to dissolution on the livid waters
fuming at the rocks that stand their ground
and offer shelter to the fish.
                                    Another season
is in the air and the black heart of the creek
is humming a sobering tune. A touch of blue
here a touch of green there: boulders disperse
a burnt sienna light to mellow the crisp
colours with which autumn defies winter.
The young maples too are burrowing between
stones for the sweetness of another season
beyond the ice age that returns each year.
You cannot see the water striders: they know
the creek is the bridge across all seasons.

3. Tom Thomson's Jackpine

Bent but never broken by the brute winds
and weathers of this northland the solitary
jackpine towers over lichen-crusted rocks
where a forest fire once gave life to its seed.
Its gnarled hands now reach over the hills
blueing deep into the citreous green twilight
trailing the sun on its retreat over the horizon
from where its fires can still touch the pine's
slender fingers. The belted kingfisher has gone
who dove from its branches with a rattle
and a splash to catch the slippery fish.
                                        Darkness
is rising from its roots and will soon grey the air
to black that's already trembling with the hoot
of the great horned owl perched out of sight
to ambush some hapless nocturnal. And yet
the light is at peace with the tree and the lake.
Calmly it amplifies the beryline silence brooding
on the waters where Tom's spirit rests forever
alongside the sky stretched out in the shadow
of the jackpine that holds heaven and earth
together in an embrace encompassing the hills
the lake, the seasons,
                        and the void that fills
the dark spaces between them and infinity.

4. J.E.H. MacDonald's Birches

Waterlogged they lean over the pond
closing ranks to form a white palisade
against the inevitable fall. Outside, the season
presses its advantage with a wave of orange
and ochre that augurs a quick dying.
Inside, beavers have dammed a creek
to raise water levels against the coming ice.
On the stillness of their pond, fall has entered
and engaged the birches behind their defences,
and they have plunged their spiked trunks
into the sky and the pond from which they draw
their strength, though the seasons travel on
the light, and below its rufous-polished mirror
the water is gnawing at their roots to prepare
for them a death by rotting.
                              Deadwood defines
the edge of the pond where a patch of sky is
bluer than the sky itself, as though you were
looking from the shadow into the light, watching
a world from under a dark shingled roof
to realize that up and down in nature (or
in art) are not even a matter of perspective.

5. Arthur Lismer's Pine

Grey grey grey — the rocks the bark the clouds streaked
with tints of mole and moose, yet the struggle of this aging
tree is passionate as the seasons it has endured. Bent
and twisted it stands stripped of its ever but not forever
green that was home to waxwings and warblers,
squirrels and raccoons, through many a luminous summer.
A few puffs of fusty green at the old pine's periphery
still needle the sky whose burden its muscular body
and limbs bear in silence, its roots firmly planted
in the rock formations they fissured, broke and heaved
in their youth.
                    Generations of woodpeckers and winter
storms will labour to bring down this tree towering
over the landscape, its twin trunks raised like arms
poised to hurl a boulder defiantly at the wind
that agitates the lake. Hissing bluegreen waters
assail the fuscous grey area of the pine's dying
that commands land and sky.
                              A touch of orange
at the core of the broken mother trunk, intimations
of pale blue between louring clouds, and the promise
of fresh green deep in the forests on the distant purple
hills plot the perennial return of all that is mortal.

6. *Lawren Harris' Deadwood*

An aureate light tempers this landscape
where nothing else is alive. Ice ages cramped
the earth into rock shorn of any vestige
of the grasses and trees whose roots once stirred
its dark heart. Isles of stone float in the still
water like the backs of giant turtles petrified
in their sleep.
                        Perhaps the aquamarine air
will encourage lichen to scale their slate humps.
The clouds are abstractions of a time
when water was the stuff of life. All that is left
of the ancient meadows and forests, the creatures
that fared and feared in them, are fossils—
and a single tree stump. Gutted and charred
by lightning, by wind and weather polished
grey and soft as the cloud bank above, it stands
tall between ultramarine water and a golden promise
the sky hasn't kept on earth. Frost split and rain
gouged its trunk and left it a broken mouth
lamenting solitude and corruption with a howl
that's opened the heavens to a burst of light.

7. Emily Carr's Forest

They lean their bronzed bodies like surf
riders into the long hollow of a colossal green
wave that has overwhelmed the sky and left it
a hint of azure in the verdant dark. This sea
brooks no opposition. The force that churns
this fawn and foliage coloured world
engulfs all in its swirling arboreal mystery:
balsam, redwood, cedar are swept up
and the minutiae of forests: cones, moss,
berries, mushrooms, broken branches,
underbrush and deadwood swallowed by this surge
of fir boughs and muscular trunks. No birdsong,
nor the crack of twigs snapping under a deer's
hoof or a bear's paw. The force that made
this forest brushed all parts into the whole:
a vortex of vegetation, creating spaces sombre
and sacramental in their silent strength, radiating
a tranquillity so monastic you can hear ancient
chants intoned softly by the umbral twilight
under the green cloistered vault humming
with praise for the magic of pure growth
a perpetual canon of evergreen voices.

Mer Bleue

The early sun is slow to melt the blue mist
night has draped over this ancient bog.
It's as though nature herself were hesitant
to expose the rare footprint of giant glaciers
to the ravages of human appropriation.

The boardwalk plunges into a blue cloud
and you wait for contours to emerge
as silhouettes morph into trees: black spruce,
tamarack, white birch—dwarfs, all of them,
but triumphant over acid constraints.

8,000 years have turned the purified water
of an ice age toxic. Sphagnum moss grew soft
layer by soft layer and packed down peat
barely a millimetre a year for a domed bog
fragrant with rosemary, laurel and Labrador tea.

Delicately, dawn's fingers lift blue veils above
the bulrushes and ignite their spiked candles.
Swaying on a reed, a redwinged blackbird calls
from the heart of stillness to proclaim
his mating rights across the bustling realm.

The dappled pads of miniature lilies
undulate gently in the clear, umber waters.
Boreal peatland, spacious and open as tundra,
for the mind to stretch out and embrace
the communion of all that struggles to survive.

A once mighty river subsided here in time
draining west and east between creek and brook
leaving two islands of sand on clay foundations
where pine and maple took root and beavers
still bite through bark and xylem into the heart-

wood of trembling aspen to bring them down
and build dams and lodges to secure their lives
and their litter. Shelter is sanctuary here
for the spotted turtle sliding its black carapace
mute between cattails and cottongrass,

sanctuary also for the bruised spirit of a creature
battering itself with the city's raucous banalities
—sanctuary granted in the rich silence
woven from the furtive murmurings
of muskrat and dragonfly, wind and water.

The boardwalk takes you to the heart of the bog.
Stand still and listen—hear the vociferous silence
beneath the surface hush. How quickly the city slips
into forgetting and leaves you to search for a home
in this precarious and uncertain world!

It's as though you were transported
to a boreal landscape in the distant past.
You almost expect to come upon a family
of triceratops grazing among the low brushwood
that punctuates the timeless heather surround.

Nine varieties of orchids blossom furtively
among the accommodating sphagnum moss,
but silver birches grow stunted and frail here.
Only oligotrophs survive the acid test of Mer Bleue
where two sand ridges point to the future.

Smell the generative decay at the margins of life
and death. This bog can preserve bodies
for millennia. Wetlands were the boundary
evolution took aeons to cross beyond the sea's
freedoms to accept the challenges of the sky.

Walk the boardwalk into the past and inhale
the peace that comes with belonging. You are
a bridge between many worlds, a link in a living
chain that reaches from before the Cambrian
marshes beyond the Holocene extinction.

The water barely moves. Only the rains feed
the aquatic exchanges with flora and fauna
that favour blueberry and leatherleaf shrubs,
tufted sedges, bog-cotton and bog-cranberries
in an intricate symbiosis of bacteria and plant.

A solitary pair of mallards drifts among reeds
causing shallow ripples to fan out and subside.
The sun is bearing down now on the city
just over the horizon. Night will restore
the integrity of flower and leaf, claw and wing.

My Garden in Four Stages

1.

My garden is fully edible;
it grows the yinyang of nutrition.

If you can tell the weeds from the feeds
you are certifiably human, all too human.

You like carrots, potatoes and peas;
other creatures prefer milkweed and thistles.

Groundhogs eat everything that sprouts
and shoots—except humans.

Not Eden, but Eaton's
mail order catalogue

used to provide pioneers
with all the tools they needed.

Nowadays not one of their spades
would fetch a single cup of coffee.

In the intemperate zone gardens
grow lima instead of coffee beans.

The berries are mostly for the birds
like the cherries in the orchard.

2.

Frankly, I'm partial to Zen gardens
where you can pattern stones to flower;

they are independent of the seasons
and let you go with the flow.

You can meditate at thirty below
and hibernate in summer when things grow.

That's why I leave a patch for pebbles
to allow imagination its spiritual revels.

All you need is a rake and a mind
to farm a garden of stones.

So long as you can dispense with reason,
it'll bear fruit in every season.

3.

When dinosaurs ruled
the whole planet was a garden.

Then an asteroid struck
and put an end to all that.

But the gardens grew back
even richer than before —

till *Homo sapiens* struck
and earth ran out of luck:

we're paving the planet over;
developers are in clover.

Nature doesn't care a monkey's fart
about politics, philosophy or art.

She will grow her garden back and better
as the climate gets hotter and wetter,

and we end up the size of a chickadee
in a future jungle's crowded canopy

or as crabs crawling at the bottom of the sea
in an octopus's garden to be or not to be.

4.

In the meantime in summer
cucumber and zucchini lunge

with fat green fingers for tomatoes
that have grown apple cheeks.

They beg for pepper, salt, spices and oil
to be exalted in salad, sauce or stew

breeding poems, dreams and meditations too
before returning peristaltic to the soil.

They leave a mouth-watering taste behind
along with a lot of perennials in the mind.

That's how gardens transcend lunch and dinner:
the neocortex not the duodenum is the winner.

The Gentle Art of Fishing

Fishing, he said to the astonished fish,
is a natural form of meditation,
an exercise in peace and tranquillity,
a civilized, gentle, healing occupation.

But the fish failed in their murky depth
to appreciate such noble sentiments,
occupied, as they were, with finding and not
becoming food in their natural element.

So the fisherman talked to himself as he was
wont to do seeing only his own reflection
in the water, thus proving his point that fishing
is a gentle, civilized form of self-satisfaction.

Let your mind, he told himself, drift
along with the boat, the hidden hook,
line and sinker, and watch the sun spread
an aureate patina on the tranquil brook.

No need to worry about the fish biting
so long as you pulled the live worm snug
and gentle over the hook like a mini condom,
leaving half to dangle for a nibble and a tug.

The morning breeze may ripple the surface
raising a pucker on the lips of a cloud
strolling in slow motion across the water
whose gentle wash makes a muttering sound.

Meditate now on the shimmering membrane
that separates water peacefully from the air,
its undulations a measure of the tranquillity
that embraces and follows you everywhere —

till you feel the tug and pull of the line,
the rod bends, a fish has taken your bait:
the wriggling worm has done its duty;
hook and net now determine the fish's fate.

The broken jaw, the lacerated mouth
are cause now for wholesome meditation —
the fish gasping his last for water,
his sleek body convulsed in desperation.

What nobler purpose here on earth
than for dumb, lowly animals like fish
to be accepted in human society
and celebrated as a succulent dish!

A blunt blow to the head ends it all —
oh, gentle peace that comes with civilization!
Gutted, deboned, filleted and fried —
the fish is proof of our gentle occupation.

We devour them full of genuine praise
for their tender flesh, served by the cook
with parsley and lemon not just for taste
but for that sublime, mouth-watering look.

Of course the fish might have preferred to go on
roaming our lakes and rivers — who can say?
They're dumb and mute, but we live in a democracy
where the loudest and sharpest have their way.

Thus the gentle art of fishing triumphs over nature,
the fruit of superior intellect and imagination.
And in their own inimitable way the fish share,
vicariously, both the meal and the meditation.

No Romance This

It's as though the flames that consumed
the house I built into the forest, also burnt
my pen. Or did I burn my fingers trying
to create a harmony that can never be
more than a passing serendipity
of what we dream of what we know
of what we desire of what we do?
Above the hot horizons of these summer nights
hovers the Fata Morgana of my yearning.

More than a hundred times this planet
has turned around itself, spinning on its ice toes
as it swings from equinox to solstice
in a dizzying round-dance of stars.
And yet I have not been moved
to put pen to paper to celebrate
what must be celebrated if death is not
to have dominion of us all before time,
before my time, is up, and yours and yours.

They call it romantic when you can feel
the strength of a tree beneath its bark.
I've just been to the cedar groves of Lebanon,
leaned against rough trunks to sense the pulse
of a more enduring life, inhaled the fragrance
of a fragile peace restored. But to the south
in an adjacent land, where the desert threatens
to bury a people's heart, I felt the ground shake
under the angry blows of bombs and missiles.

They call it romantic when you can hear
the birds sing their morning hymn to a world
that gave them wings. My wings and yours
are in the mind. They take us to a world
of music and love where Jehovah's children
grind Allah's children into the hot sand
under the chains of their tanks, or blast them
into eternity with intelligently designed weapons.
Our wings take us higher than birds can fly.

They call it romantic when you can see
the wind undulate a ripe wheat field as though
it were an ocean of gold. That same gold bug-eyes
our lust for power so that neighbour can kill
neighbour in a super-race delirium. Show me
an analogue to Palestine or Rwanda among any
of our fellow-creatures not so blessed with virtue
and wisdom, and I'll pick up my pen again
to lament with the trees, the birds, and the wind.

I am a wounded animal. So are you. The wound is
nature's. The gash between her legs and the sword
in my groin. We are given life to want
what is denied us. That it be everlasting.
We take life to that end. That is the wound
from which we bleed to death. No romance this.
Yet our fellow-travellers rejoice. With fearful eyes.
And my pen wants to rejoice with them. But my heart
is uneasy. I catch the sharp claws in my neighbour's eye.

It's those claws that set my pen in motion again.
I've seen them in the eyes of lions too. *Ex ungue leonem.*
Savages too can be noble. I learnt to read as a child
the writing of bombs and bullets on the walls of houses.
And I learnt to listen to music: my father at the piano
and the birds in a king's forest. I'm still learning
to blend blast and melody in a song that celebrates
as it laments a world that lives by dying. How to read
in the viscera of the players the splendour of the play.

Music in the Rafters

(Brahms' Piano Quartet opus 60 at Festival Alexandria, Ontario)

1. Allegro non troppo

Nothing prepared this country barn
for such a dark tempest in C minor.
The piano storms into the hushed afternoon
to rage between the violin and the viola
where a heart is torn apart by the split love
for a friend battling to keep his mind
above madness, and for his friend's wife.

The heat is so oppressive you can feel
the sun spread out on the roof like a jelly-
fish, the light forcing its tentacles inside
between barnboards. A bitter dispute between
the cello and the violin tears apart the passion
of youth this August afternoon as it confronts
the sterner discipline of music in the rafters.

Nothing prepared this country audience
for so much pain and yearning in a summer
barn. Flies are driven frantic by four voices
tearing melodies apart, flinging the pieces
into distant keys, the melancholy cello as
impetuous as the piano and the viola contesting
the high-pitched romance of the violin.

The heat is palpable and leaves a bitter taste.
Robert Schumann leaped into a river to drown
the mad voices that tore his music apart.
Brahms walking by the river stringing melodies
on the rack of love battling love. Nothing
can settle the dark and desperate disputes
of the heart, not even a final C minor chord.

2. Scherzo

So intense is the heat
the air breaks into sweat.

They fished Robert from the river
when Clara was pregnant
with a seventh child.

Which way shall the heart turn
in its dark search? Which passage
of love or music shall it take
to reach what little light there is

in fulfilment? Young Johannes stayed
while Robert's mind unravelled behind bars;
not even her piano could console Clara.

The players are in a sweat now
so intense is the anguish in the music.

Their fingers slide
on strings and keys
to reconcile the logic
of passion with what
the heart has learned
two decades later
of fate and the muses.

3. Andante

Slowly softly
the light begins to sing
in the cello
raises from its strings
a melody
that blossoms in E major
tenderly slowly
lifts its voice beyond
the centuries
Johannes
sings his love
for Clara
here and now
fills this barn
this summer
afternoon
with yearning
till Clara responds
slowly
gently together
the cello and the violin
lift their love
beyond desire
to become music
in the rafters
the passion a melody
twenty years later
a memory
in the piano bittersweet
love
transfigured in the singing
light
filters through barnboards

slowly
tenderly startles
our hearts
to tears
for nothing
prepared us for
the sublime
strings can pluck
from the flesh's
adversity.

The ash tree outside
presses its leaves
against the window
and filters the light
green into the last
gentle measure
of love
consummated
in music.

4. *Finale*

The violin now lifts the afternoon up high
a deeper light threads a hue of happiness
across the shadows of Clara in a minor key
of love come to fruition in this barn.
But someone stalks the piano, something
sinister hammers hard and insistent—fate
syncopating our heartbeat, the same
fate that spared Robert almost
one hundred and fifty years ago
the final dissolution and despair
involves and overwhelms us all.

The shadows have lengthened. Darkly
they fall across the audience across
the players across melodies that contain
turmoil in the heart resigning the pain
to an almost serene sorrow nothing prepared
this country barn for, and nothing,
not two decades nor two centuries,
can erase: Robert died and the lovers
moved apart into their own worlds
their own memories their own music.

Outside, the sun is mellowing in the grass.
The passion of a youth has matured
into melodies beyond any age. Love surrendered
is not love lost—but is it oh is it not
worth a quartet? Six quartets? The piano
chromatically brings the shadows down to scale.
The heat inside still tastes as salty
as the melodies strung between the rafters.
Johannes' emotions are composed now and
climax in a final, unanswerable C major cry.

Deep Sky Observations

(for Leo Enright)

The telescope as optic
fishing-rod:
the eye casts about
in the black meandering
stream of night
to catch a fleeing star
or haul a galaxy
from the deep
sky to still
a hunger of the mind.

Curiosity flies barbed
at the end of light
years across space
breaks the surface
of perception and plunges
for a strike — the retina tenses
a line of thought jerks
aeons into vision:

—M 13
a school of suns
slides into focus
a globular cluster of fire
blossoms a million times
brighter than high noon
each a nuclear furnace
to sear the imagination

—M 15
stellar arms flailing
whirl a pool of stars
into a galactic wheel
that reels time in
to the birth of winter
at an eocene catastrophe

—M 57
where a dying star
dances in a ring
nebula of metastable atoms
more rarefied than a vacuum
yet luminous enough
to pitch a thousand years
of light here bluegreen

We are adrift
in a river of darkness
glittering with the debris
of a primal blast
that tempered the void
to the blood's illusions
you and I observe

far flung constellations
the wreckage of cosmic
accidents the swelling
and shrinking of stars
burning to dust older
than the planets older
than the whole solar dream

fragments of a unity
that became a flash
and broke into flames
shooting out in all
directions stretching
a fist into an infinite
night forcing the void
to retreat before the universe

a balloon dilating with the speed
of electrons, filling with blank
space, stars streaking away
along sightlines leading
nowhere in no time at all
till we hold nothing
against our solitude
but the invisible light
against the cutting edge
of what we call
eternity.

Skies and Solitudes

Skies tempestuous as the rage of ancient gods
yet at once tranquil as interstellar space.

Calmly clouds tear themselves to shreds.
Like full and solitary sails they drift
across the blue infinity of our minds.

Somewhere at the dark centre of our selves
a screening-room where we sit in silence
and watch the ceaseless dance of colours,

trying to see the faces and read the signs
that tell us we are not alone in our solitude.

Sky/Wave

(a painting by Arlette Francière)

A blue tsunami unleashed, then arrested as it crests after
sweeping the canvas clean of tormented rocks and clouds,
masks of troubled spirits that ghost the landscapes this artist's
pen and brush have magicked into the principalities of her art.
Stillness has settled on a world in motion, a blue moment
of meditation at the core of unending transformation.

An artist's sightlines encompass everything, the whole
spectrum from the right of the heart to the left
of darkness whence this blue wave rises. Reaches
above the green horizon, beyond the turbulence
of despair and desire. Attains a tranquillity of spaces
inhabited only by themselves and by what might be.

Blueness is a cosmic gesture here. The hollow of a hand
holding a promise of eternity it cannot keep. A dome
to shelter the mind stretching to infinity where music
blasts from the deep outside human range to resonate
the heavens. An ocean rearing to lift us into its blue
exuberance to become one with air, salt and water.

In this hyperbole of streaming blues, oil, colour and canvas
become one too, a membrane permeable to the inner eye
only. What happens here is a grand entrance to a warren
where the flecked ground slides like green lava beneath
the surface. We are drawn into deepening shades. Ultramarine
the artist's dare to follow the light to the end of the tunnel.

2. away from home ...

There Are No Ends

I have felt the flow of many oceans lure me
beyond the surf where the sea foams at the mouth
chewing rock and roots, felt its ebb draw me
below the sea's spit and spume by wind and weather
jumbling surfaces. An undertow too strong to resist,
too ancient for the neocortex to reason into words
has pulled me down to the dark centre of beginnings
—and there, by the flicker of phosphorescent fish,
I saw the circle close in the hull of a ship's wreck.
We are the sea's, and as such we are at its beck.

The foundered ship is but a prodigal return.
I hear the distant drumming waves in my heart
though we have moved far from the sea, dragging
its weight and its salts from species to species
and to the moon. We have transubstantiated water
into worlds of steel and concrete, music and microchips,
that seem a triumph over nature. Yet we must
each replenish our cental of saltwater day by day
and make singing the sea to the sky life's norm.
We are the water within the wave and the wave's form.

I have drifted in the waters of many oceans
and felt the waves form at the core of calm seas.
Everything is forever moving, forever becoming
something else. In the cosmic recycling plants
that mixed the elements which produced us, water
is nature's strategy for transformations. The sun
draws from the wave the drop that must pass your lips
for you to see, hear, feel—just for the blood to flow
and for synapses enabling love and poetry to grow.
And little will man—or woman, come to that—

how we came to travel these waterways of thought
and perception. The trillions of particles chance
compounded into, say, Plato or Cleopatra have long
scattered far and wide again and may even now
in their countless manifestations be stirring the hand
that writes these lines. Passion and wisdom too
are strategies of transformation. There are no ends
to justify beginnings. We are passages between worlds
past and future, and none of us can ever bring back
Know what he shall dream when drawn by the sea's wrack.

By the Pacific Ocean (off Kauai)

Even calm this ocean is never peaceful, never at rest,
never smooth enough to mirror a passing cloud,
never so silent that you can hear the koa trees hum—
always it churns and surges running relentlessly ashore.

Ceaseless sea, pawing this island with coral claws
like a savage and insatiable lover, mating the earth
with deep-mouthed cries, waves slapping the coast's thighs
as the surf shoots foam-flecked into dark coves.

Exhausted the sea turns tides and floats on its back,
a woman now, wide open for the wind to ravish across reefs.
The ocean's violence is quick and sudden, its intimacies sheer,
except when night falls and stars cover it with silver damask.

The passion the wind stirs up deep inside the waters is raw
as a tsunami: its shorebreak crushes boats and rocks,
sweeps us off our feet and takes our breath away
before subsiding in the sand with a shiver and a sigh.

It took aeons for the ceaseless water wheels of sea and sky
to bank the fire at this planet's core and cool molten rock down
to the temperature of trees and flowers, birds and mammals,
making a new world for the ocean's emigrants to settle.

We're born yet in the sea of our mothers where our hearts
pick up the beat of tides and learn to love by the waves—
rhythms, rolling, falling and rising. Once airborne we set sail
on the chancy waters of an ocean that forgives nothing.

We moved closer to the stars at the price of carrying
a piece of the sea inside us, and still it salts our kisses
and tears, though it has long turned sweet and sanguine.
We cannot return to the sea and sing, like the whales

who reclaimed their watery home and breach the waves now
with their whole weight exuberant in its buoyancy, its element,
while we must ride the force that rolls the heaving waters
into green spinning furious funnels, at the risk of drowning.

Between the pull of the moon and the push of continental plates
vast schools of fish shift and turn as though on command
their silver flashing deep in murky halls of cold liquid glass
where amino acids were first put to the test and came to life.

Tonight I understand what the waters holler across lava cliffs,
the tales, the legends they recite in the sand, of ships and voyages,
of storms and floods, of the ebb and flow of all things: we share
the tides with the oceans, with the stars and with our lovers.

At night the ceaseless sea drums and bellows at the solitude
as though calling us back to the fluid transparency of a world
we left a thousand million years ago for greener pastures,
for the promise of a greater freedom, and for a chance to fly.

Something lures me to dive into the waters and dare the riptides,
some need to feel the softness at the beginning and find a clue,
but the breakers tumble and toss me and the wind lashes
hissing spray across my face as I lie back in the cradle of life.

New Year in Bali

(for Myrna)

Something holier and more ancient
than their most ancient gods
summons the people of this island
to renew the year. From every village
they walk down festive roads mile
after dusty mile bringing the suns fire
reified in fruit and flowers to Shiva
and the gods of rice and water by the sea.

Under *janur* decorations hung low
from tall sleek bamboo poles they come:
the men in sun-yellow sarongs, immaculate
white smocks, the *destar* bright and jaunty
in their black hair. Their smile only
hints at their embarrassment: they have come
to submit their manhood to a larger force
stirring dark and foam-flecked in the sea.

The women delicate as blossoms
in lace blouses topping their sarongs,
colourful as birds of paradise, a single
hibiscus in their hair: erect and graceful
as palm trees they carry bowls of fruit
and flowers on their heads, moving
with ease here where they are at home
sharing the ancient rituals with the sea.

Legs crossed and hands folded they sit
smiling in the sand, women and men,
old and young, offering their *bhakti*
to the dancing gods with shell and lotus.
Innocent of the violence lurking in a faith
more ferocious than their gentle embrace
of all that lives, their sightlines don't include
those determined to enforce their delusions.

Kindness has no defences against treachery.
Soon terror will be imported here from abroad.
Already the makers of bombs are planning
in secret to strike at the heart of their peace.
For now Bali celebrates. Boys and girls turn
to face the waves, set fruit and flowers
afloat in small coconut-leaf vessels
and watch the tide feed them to the sea.

In return the water blesses them
as wave after wave rolls in and over
like the wheel of death and rebirth
from which they can escape only when
they understand that they are the waves
and that sand and self are one with the sea
and the fragrant smoke of incense they burn
for their gods to please and protect them.

Venice

1.

Mirage in a lime-green lagoon translucent
as the dawn that brushes gold across

the mist slowly the silhouettes of roofs
and spires fade from silence into view

buildings mysteriously manifest façades
acquire sparkle colour grandeur

become mansions palaces churches
whose blind windows look squarely

at the sun in a celestial ghost town
that defies the disbelieving eye — a city

is born in shimmering undulations of water
and light glides into marble and terra cotta

till stone dreams gold and Venice
wakes to the muffled call of foghorns.

2.

The sun now pours orange light
into the canals and a stiff breeze
whitecaps the water as Canaletto did.

Stone bridges lace a patchwork
of islets across a water net
that holds Venice together.

The city map is a flow chart
of the circulation of the sea
whose tides pulse through a web

of arteries that has fed its citizens
pageants, spices, fruit, silk and song
down the sedulous passage of time.

An ancient people once found refuge
in these marshes, driving wooden stakes
to build a narrow escape into a dream

worthy of a goddess born in a conch
and risen from the waves to be crowned
by the sun queen of all the world's cities.

3.

Serenissima! The very air here vibrates
with the glories of line and colour
and stone flexes lustrous as light:
mansions as mysterious as their absentee
owners, their ochre façades adorned
with pillared balconies of Istrian stone
white as summer clouds drifting
on emerald waters between candy-striped
anchor posts and the black dance of
gondolas concave as crescent moons.

The linear geometry of brick ruddy
against arabesques in pale stucco,
the arched nobility of Gothic peaking
in a Byzantine crest, ornamental arches
and archivolts, isorhythmic tracery
in red Verona marble, green gardens
hidden behind crenellated walls—all lend
elegance to Renaissance determination
muscling oriental grace into stone for
a proud setting to life's tragicomedies.

And hovering above the undulating fields
of crimson-tiled roofs, livid in a blue Adriatic
sky, guarding their mosaic splendour
the domes of San Marco's Basilica:
there among parapets and pilasters, crockets,
capitals and cornices, stone saints yearn
in their aedicules for a world beyond the wind
and rain that have long disfigured them
where the lonely heart's quest ends
in bliss that is more than a golden memory.

4.

In the pale saffron light of his palace
the doge throws his ring into the harbour
to renew the city's solemn vows to the sea,
their union more intimate year by year.

Seagulls scatter in the sky like large white
blossoms a gust of wind has lofted in the air;
they shriek as though the passionate aria
of an operatic gondolier had excited them to ecstasy.

Not far away Wagner first heard the plaint
his shepherd pipes on his horn to lament
the tragedy of true love, heard also the last
dirge to mourn his own death in Venice.

Stone becomes music as the Rialto bridge
swings across the Grand Canal with one leap
carrying Antonio's thirteen arches shimmering
on the tide like a surge of strings by Vivaldi.

White masks and black cloaks move
furtively among bright coloured costumes
of carnival revellers borrowing other lives
to the tune of flutes, guitars and drums.

At Easter a procession crosses the piazza
as stately as Bellini painted it, except for
the crowds pushing and the smell of garlic,
wine and fresh bread lurking in the alleys.

But a sea breeze finds you anytime anywhere
and ruffles your hair as it frisks, fondles you
shamelessly, and you taste its salt on the air.
A kiss here is ancient music in the mouth.

5.

Yet year by year Venice
sinks inexorably deeper
into black wafting weeds
till the union of sea
and stone is absolute
and only memories gild
the waters measuring
the transience of things
routinely to a fault.

Already tourists drift
in the black coffins
of lacquered gondolas
through the city as though
it were a floating museum,
its inhabitants guardians
of a golden past,
its treasures archaeological,
its songs for sale.

But it is not only the wind
that still sings in the streets
and the waters of Venice:
signorie and *popolani* still
bring their newborn to the font
with a Gloria and with a Lacrimosa
they bury their dead
across a bridge of boats
on the isle of San Michele.

In a dark and dank hall
of the Scuola di San Rocco
Tintoretto has painted
triangles into a composition
that contains all the world's
woes in a panorama
so luminously human
it eclipses corruption
in a rapture of art.

6.

Evening is pouring liquid gold over domes
and spires, pinnacles and finials, into the canals.

The four bronze horses of San Marco stare unseeing
across the piazza at the light loitering in its colonnades.

Beneath their hooves the gold mosaics of another age
flush with a sudden glow and then slowly dim.

At the clock tower the Magi wait in hiding for the Moor
to strike the hour for their gaudy puppet dance.

From below the horizon the sun burns the city's skyline
hard-edged into an orange ground blueing eastwards.

A moment of splendour passes as stone oozes darkness
into palaces and churches, streets and waterways.

At the foot of the campanile swarms of pigeons flap
their wings as though to dispel the intrusion of dusk.

Night rises like an expanding bubble of glass
blown blue black and full of stars from the sea:

a vast dark cosmic balloon to lift Venice glittering
into a universe of golden dreams inside our hearts.

San Miguel Sketchbook
(a Mexican suite for Angelica)

1. Mañanita

In the *jardin* the spindled Indian
trees shake the last remnants
of night from their green plumage:
a black cloud of *urracas*
rises shrill as magpies
and sweeps across the plaza
like the shadow of a hand.

Now the town tolls
its many bells in the towers
of a score of churches, scattering
their chimes across empty roof-tops,
languidly, as if the very belfries
were half asleep, the hours
they keep lost in a dream.

The morning rings softly
in the wind's mansion, the sky
opens its gates to let out
the first light to graze
like a herd of goats, relentless,
horns turning to gold,
in the cactus-studded hills.

Slowly the day climbs
over the mountain ridge,
struggles down thorny
broken slopes and dizzily
descends the cobbled streets
with the milkman and his mule
delivering a cool sun.

2. Blind Beggar

The sharp and slanted
rays of the early sun
have pinned him
to his shadow
on the cracked wall
like a rare specimen
of some singular
eyeless species
in a run-down museum.

Daily he taps his
way to this same
spot, stepping
warily alert
across the cobbles
as though searching with
his cane for treasure
on some lonely pebbled
beach.

But the sea
he edges is behind
his permanently lowered
eyelids; it teems
with disembodied voices
and the feel of things
unseen.

A gash in
the pink plaster
of the cold church
wall touches him
and confirms his place
in the world beyond
colour just ten steps
from Pedro's tin and
copper stand with its
tinkle of bells and
clatter of pans, brass
handles and steel
knives, that tell him
of the bustle and bargains
of every market day.

I've seen his eyes
in Michoacán, young
and golden, in a Tarascan
face long before
Cortez' greed
crushed Moctezuma's
tribe — or else
they flashed hatred
in a fierce Chichimec
band fighting
bow and arrow
the cannons of Juan
the barefoot Franciscan
come to open native
eyes to the blinding
light of his rapacious
Spanish gods.

Time has ploughed
the beggar's face
and the ravens of hunger
have picked clean
the furrows where want
has taken root
and a whole people
suffer in the dark
shadow of his shabby
sombrero.

The cold
stone against his
back supports him
and the sun drops
the hours like gold
coins into the cup
he cradles close
to his chest as though
he were of two
minds about alms
and begging
about being there
at the edge of a dark
sea of chatter
that spits an occasional
peso at him.

The sounds
and smells of the town
include him, give him
the news of the street
and when the sun
like a parting friend
takes its warm hand
off his shoulder
they show him
the way home.

3. The Market

The market squats in the square
outside Nuestra Señora de la Salud
where Juan de Gamarra once taught
the body is nothing to the mind:

because you think you are god is
good. Cornucopia of flowers and
fruit overflowing into every cross
and side street, down Insurgentes

as far as the public library, stalls
lined up shoulder to shoulder
copious with oranges and pecans,
avocados and cane, peppers

beans, papaya—amongst them squat
on naked flagstones women whom
labour and deprivation have worn
down early to old and untutored

age, scraping thorns off cacti,
begging you with their eyes dark and
stoic in the hushed stained-dust
shade to buy their handful of

vegetables for the sake of their
shackful of ragtag children
whose bloated bellies teach them
nothing but the crafts of survival.

For native children the goodies
at the market are bedtime stories.
Too many cold stars have filled
their lungs with bronchial slime.

Barefoot and snotnosed they wheeze
wordlessly begging for pesos,
their minds a hungry grin
1,870 m above Gamarra's philosophy.

Between orchids, roses and hibiscus
young men hawk wares too
cheap and plastic for the rich
gods of America who think

they are, however, good enough
for primitive consumption: plastic
shoes plastic clothes plastic watches
plastic statues of the Virgin — all

as worthless as the peso and the *gringo*
promises of wealth. Bulletin:
They're taking Mexico to market
to teach them the value of junk.

Trust the old Indian woman
squeezing oranges all day
blending their sweetness with raw
eggs and bananas, and handing you

a drink with such delicious pride
you know the spirit of her ancestors
lives — lives in the unlettered
hands that pluck the strings

of a guitar or chisel a chac-mool
from stone or hammer copper
into shapes to make the sun
dance round and round

the bright colours of shawls
and ponchos, round the baskets
of nuts, fruit and flowers
the light lured from the recalcitrant

soil, and round his people
who think with their bodies and are,
therefore, as good as the earth
they bring to this market.

4. *High Noon and After*

At the apex of the day the sun burns
a fierce hole right above the spire
of the parish church into the blue globe

that cups San Miguel like an alchemist's
retort melting the very stone down to gold
even the conquistadores couldn't pillage.

The pastel-coloured houses blister in the heat
that turns cobbles into live coals and
makes the narrow streets a labyrinth of fire.

The light licks the last coolness
even from the flagstone in the patios
where tropical flowers thirst for shade.

There's no escape but a siesta
though indoors too the sultry air smells
singed and beds break into sweat.

Only the thick, windowless church walls
preserve a stale frostiness where the town's
five patron saints rest in perpetuity.

In the park a young couple furtively explores
intimacies that match the temperature:
the cicadas are sizzling in their blood.

Lake and river are too far to bring relief
from this summer furnace. If only one could
inhabit the interior of a water melon.

5. The Parish Church of St. Michael

In a maze of pillars and pilasters,
towers and turrets, the patron saint
still grasps the lance
which slew the pagan
dragon that ruled this land
for sunnier gods
before Michael led his celestial
ragtag army to Tenochtitlan.

Miraculously
pagan blood proved to be
as red as any Spaniard's.
But rain leaches blood from stone
and centuries of it left
pink the masonry of La Parroquia
where the conquered met their conquerors
on more equal terms.

A Chichimec hand made a cross here
as elaborate as a cathedral.
Tutored only by the architecture
of his own body and by an inner eye
that saw the strains and stresses
in all things the native builder
drew his designs in sand
with sticks and stones mastered
his picture postcard masters.

Behind a grudging gothic mask
the ancient gods of Mexico smile still:
the mystery of sun, rain and seed
have here become sensible
living stone and el Señor de la Conquista
was taught to dance in it
to the music of *concheros*.

Even in the clammy gloom inside
the church the cornstalk god dances,
performs before images of the Virgin
and impersonates Ecce Homo, casting
a cold eye on the crypt
that once impressed an alien emperor
where now the ghosts of many rest
whose dreams have long come to dust.

To atone for their nightmares the rich
and noble gave gold rings chains
bracelets brooches to melt into La Luz,
the bell that tolls now
from its tumid tower, its tongue tempered
by native gold calls the poor,
clear and sonorous as the light
to bring their miseries to be blessed.

The pious mask of La Parroquia remains
serene behind the iron bars
that stake out the atrium;
unflinching it confronts the evergreen
succulence of ficus trees in the *jardin*.
The bell tolls and forces masks of piety
on rebellious blood. The pink stone shivers.
The light comes in waves of heat and dust.

6. Fiesta

On feast days even the light sings
and dances through the festooned town,
throws kisses and flowers from doorways
and windows, polishes ancient copper
faces till all care is removed, eyes
sparkle and hearts sing in their cage:
I don't want silver
and I don't want gold,
I want to stay young
and never grow old.

Sun and passion flowers, woven
between marigolds and dyed tortillas
across frames of reed, pattern mats
of *cucharillos* whose green leaves spoon
laughter out to whistles and balloons
to celebrate old rhythms and new tunes:
Swing the stick,
swing the stick,
hit the piñata
and hit it quick!

Flutes haunt the scarlet dancers
and drums move them to ritual
combat, feathers flying, headbands
flashing for Our Lady of Guadeloupe
triumphs over Oxomoco's dark arts
though the mariachi bands know better:
I don't want silver
and I don't want gold,
I want to stay young
and never grow old.

A bright-coloured bird of papier-mâché
with a clay pot belly full of candy
hangs glutted above the blindfolded boy,
swings this way and that, high and low,
dodges the broomstick that hits only air
while young and old tease and cheer:
Swing the stick,
swing the stick,
hit the piñata
and hit it quick!

The spirit of each season gives life
to all saints who honour the god
of love, play and dance: his madness
leaps across time from a monkey's leer
deep in the black heart of obsidian
and rules day and night of every fiesta.
I don't want silver
and I don't want gold,
I want to stay young
and never grow old.

The day cools off, processions snake up
the early evening, *pulque* flows, the music
grows hotter, *locos* in their devil's masks
clown evil, tequila flows, fireworks erupt
till the cobbles dance with the moon and
lovers lament the fiesta ending too soon:
Swing the stick,
swing the stick,
hit the piñata
and hit it quick!

7. Paseo at Night

Night descends and the sky
becomes a smoked-glass mirror
for Huehueteotl, the ancient fire god,
spinning his bright wheel hissing
and crackling outside the church,
setting a cross ablaze to shower
the *jardin* with sparks and screeches,
and shooting flaming arrows
straight up to explode high above
St. Michael's spires where the stars
flare inexorably beyond the moon.

Under the many-coloured rain
of fire the young circle each other,
a crowded promenade round and
round the square, two wheels
turning in opposite directions, one
inside the other—girls, arms linked
against the swagger of the boys,
guarding their secrets, passing again
and again as passion noisily sparks quips
and giggles in a mating ritual more
ancient than the gods of Teotihuacan.

The fireworks of love last no longer
than the pyrotechnics of the saints.
The moon is spreading white sheets
across the plaza, drapes them over
its trees where the *urracas* fought
to sleep in their magpie dreams, and
stretches them over the town's roofs
across the plateau up to the mountain
tops. A bell tolls unaccountably;
its muffled tongue bespeaks no hour
and dies unheeded in the ghostly streets.

Oasis

Succulent as the dark flower in your thigh
this well hides mouthfuls of rain or river
among sand-dunes shifting between sun and wind,
hoards water to succour wandering tribes
and charts the desert for traders, warriors
and lovers to travel the ancient routes
carrying the lifeblood of civilizations.

The animals quenched their thirst,
squatted down in the circle
the campfire drew in the sand
to ruminate through the night,
muttering like distant rivers
dreaming in their rocky beds
of the sea and the return to heaven.

Slowly we peeled off
the day's glare and dust,
stripped the centuries between us
of the delusions of race and class
till we were stark and naked again,
then drank coolness from cupped hands,
watching flames rekindle our eyes.

The poet's voice leaned against his camel
and surveyed the ancient tales
passing between us like caravans
laden with the spoils of war and love
which we traded with passion for a song.
Darkness reached across the stars
and threw a handful of silver into the well.

Joined at the root of night our shadows
danced about the fire, leapt hand in hand
over the moon's dagger, ran past Bedouin tents
and lay down whispering in the sand,
lost to each other in a granular void.
Dawn reassembled the desert and I found you
curled up in the riddle of a pale smile.

And still water gathers secretly at this oasis
and daubs the well's edges green enough
to mark the place where for centuries
camels squatted down and poets sang courage
to the hearts of warriors and ecstasy
to lovers riding waves of sand ashore,
their voices flying high in the desert wind.

El-Mirbed's Poets Move to Basra

From Baghdad to Basra the night
was alive with metaphors measured
by the rhythm railroad tracks
beat into trains clanking
through deserts and marshlands
through the passionate madness of poets
rushing their solitude to market.

The morning was waiting for us
at the station with its fierce light
to watch Basra put us to shame:
chanting clapping dancing
the city celebrated us
and our recalcitrant craft —
men, women and children,
their hearts cheering
in their dark eyes laughing
in a few thousand faces,
old and young, fitting together
joy, sorrow and endurance
in the improbable jigsaw puzzle
of their lives, of *our* lives,
forming an animated map of the land,
the city and the soil they will not
surrender to any foreign invader,
to any shah with or without turban.

Kurdish bands drumming the mountains
into music, Bedouin bands fluting
the desert into a dance of friendship,
whole schools of children
their innocence camouflaged
lining the streets with raptures
their uniforms cannot contain,
obelisk women in black *abayas*
their tongues undulant with the ancient
sea as they call *hewa hewa* to song,
and the soldiers, men whom war
has forced to leave the bazaars
of their youth to follow
the grim trade of killing,
applauding the singers of love
and peace — voices and instruments
a chorus ringing with the courage
of a people unvanquished by the sword.

Basra reached out to us
with countless hands festooned
with flowers and flags, dates,
laban, rosewater and sweetmeats,
welcoming us in an embrace encompassing
a planet, arms of brotherhood
reaching from the Shatt al-Arab
to the Nile and westwards across oceans
to the Mississippi up the Red River
and over northern seas to the Thames
back down the Rhine and the Danube
down the Tigris to the Shatt al-Arab —
a vast circle this people has drawn
with their blood in the sands of time
for all of us to enter and join hands
in a dance of such joy that the monster
of war must finally devour itself.

But far away the guns were not silent.
They beat the drums of destruction
as poets sang of lovers in the gardens
of their dreams ... till they too
took up the call to arms. Never
surrender to the threat of force.
The heart must choose in freedom
to be human. Utbah ibn Ghazwan,
the ancient city raised its voice
and sang to us of massacres and martyrs.
Together we mourned the death of innocents
and celebrated the endurance of a people
who want nothing but the sun
floating in across the Arabian Gulf
and the dignity of their daily lives.

The night between Basra and Baghdad
was heavy with the grief of poets
returning to a festival richer now
for the memories of sad black eyes
and children's trust, exploding shells
and hugs of friendship — all jostling
in their hearts with images of courage
and compassion as the train laboured
through the darkness carrying
the weight of senseless dying
war loads on the back of pride.

The marshes were silent. The stars
drifted among reeds. People here,
people anywhere want an end to fighting,
to bloodshed, however holy the cause.
Our journey is too short and too vital
to waste tomorrow on a whim of pride.
The train was drumming it on glittering
tracks across dark spaces into our hearts.

Manifesto in Times of War

Tell the enemy this:
that missiles can no more blow up the human spirit
than tanks can crush an idea.
Guns are the weapons of the impotent,
and I wouldn't trade one line of true poetry
for a thousand of them. The blood flowers
in a poem while bombs can only spill it.
Shrapnel can shatter glass and shred the flesh
but it cannot silence the song in a people's heart.

Tell the enemy this:
that our missiles fly on imagination's wings —
they're poems aimed to explode in the heart
with all the violence of love and compassion.
It may flatter princes to think the sword mightier
than the pen, but we have the last word.
The true poet pioneers paths of freedom
and places on the future's mouth a brotherhood kiss
with the rage of a rainstorm that makes the desert bloom.

Tell the enemy this:
that every man, woman and child wears a helmet
poets hammer from a metal harder than any steel—
the metal of their faith in creation.
You can tear a person limb from limb
but you cannot sever a song from the listening heart,
and when your missiles long rust in scrapyards
today's tears will have watered the desert
to make yesterday's laughter blossom into tomorrow's love.

Tell the enemy this: Yes,
we're still writing poems, and if your grenades
blow off our hands, we'll sing them into the future.

Letter to the Goddess of Flowers

Phoolan Devi, I never knew you   even
existed   before last night   I saw you emerge
from the water and the sun   your eyes dark   flowers
answering a father's call   away from child's play
to be a bride to   and for   a goat   and a bike.

I never even knew you could be   born a drum
but it says so   in Hindu scriptures   along with
animals *mallahs* must be beaten   and women
beaten and fucked   like drums are   banged and beaten
low-caste girls are   like you   flowers trampled by beasts.

I saw the brute   more than twice your age   and size
barter a child bride   then savage your flesh   deflower
you before   you could flower   I heard the screams
as you came to know   the blood's way   the sister-fucker
forced on you   till you lost   your heart to a whimper.

I never knew   such pain   in the flesh   could flower
into legend   only because   you picked yourself up
and walked into a freedom   bandits offered
in a wasteland not knowing hell   has no bottom
for the abused   there's always another   outrage.

I watched the lawless   though you were one of them
beat and bang you   one rapist shot   in the act
by the only lover   you had   shot in your arms
by Thakur bandits   scum of the middle-caste
they tied your hands   like a bunch of flowers

behind your back   forced your legs apart   raped you
one by one   for three days and three   nights   gangbanged
you over   and over   till your body was   nothing
but a battered bruise   and you staggered   naked
and mocked   to the village well   a broken flower.

I never knew you   could crawl back   even from such
filth and ravage   to reclaim your shattered   dignity
or that it had to be   the blood's   not the flowers'
way   you turned their rods on them   and massacred
your nightmares   to become   their bandit queen   legend.

I am writing to send   you all that   I have left:
the shame of a man's   naked desire   his power
tool to make new   worlds in the savaged flesh   only
when flowers spring   where the tears fall   we share
knowing   revenge   can never be   redemption.

So I prefer to think of you   as a true   *fleur du mal*
an avenging angel   risen   from the pit   of humiliation
to remind us   poverty is not   a matter of metaphysics
even in India   nor is the body   a drum   to be beaten
as though love were not   the only flower   in the flesh.

The Tower of Babel

yes burning their
mudpacks hard and
fast they could build
of them a tower that was
to be a city unto heaven in
the desert nomads weary of
measuring noman's land by hoof
camel tracking from oasis to oasis
wayfaring at the wind's mercy across
waves of sand that surf on the shores of
history herdsmen of goats & sowers of grain
& rice in river valleys swept too often by flood
or parched by drought the swift spears & swords
of war-faring marauders too diminished the tribe
mingled till they spoke in tongues a language of pride
that was to be the rock on which to build Babel brick by
brick bound mud slime straw into a nation leaving windows
and doors to let in the stars & keep out heat and sandstorm till
their stone mountain peaked in the sky & there they dwelled like
gods & toyed with their dreams & their designs making streets run
eastwest northsouth making justice supreme & happiness divine life
ever after became triumphant beyond sense & season beyond planets
& reason escaping the neural labyrinth to fly each to their own star soar
on wings of pride deaf to each other the language of love not reaching them

3. time weighing in the bones ...

Threescore and Ten / And Still Learning

My mother is gathering dust now in the darkness
where memory stores the remnants of life lived.
Her picture fades among the bric-a-brac of names
detached from faces, dates jumbled and disembodied,
voices whispering or crying, snatches of pleasure, reunions
encounters in uncertain places, passion and its betrayals
in dark rooms love hurts, countless farewells at train stations—
there she hangs, my mother, full-lipped and warm-eyed
forever, in a dim and discontinuous world receding year
by year, the picture of my childhood fading, like her smile.
Threescore and ten, and still learning
What to remember and what to forget,
Still learning it's absurd to divvy up the past
Into what to rejoice in and what to regret.

In that same dark gallery my father still stalks melodies
that rocked my cradle to enchanted sleep in a crude world.
Phrase by phrase and chord by chord he conjured music
from a black box where hammers were taught to sing
and dance on strings that tuned my heart to a gentler world.
Bach, Beethoven, Mozart, Brahms, Chopin and Debussy
nursed and trained me in the bittersweet joy of being alive.
I cannot hear the sound of a piano without seeing my father
's fingers run, skip, leap, across polished black and ivory tiles
in a fugue that has as many parts and keys as I have memories.
Threescore and ten, and still learning
Life, like music, is a matter of time,
Still learning that all images fade
To the ridiculous from the sublime.

The memories where once I was at home are now a labyrinth:
Strange rooms, disconnected, incongruous, their occupants departed
along dark passageways I smell my way to lovers lost and found:
Orange blossoms in Sevilla echo with the clack of castanets
in gypsy caves, the fragrance of mimosas excites my hands
to feel the naked pliance of a woman's breast, and a sea wind
salts so many moonlit nights I fall to dreaming everlasting love
and loving. A woman's scent clings to the soft hills and valleys
of her flesh, and in the shade and rustle of some furtive thrill
mingles with the musk and mould of ancient forests and tidal flats.
Threescore and ten, and still learning
We owe love and loving to death,
Still learning to celebrate the force that denies
Me all I desire till my last breath.

Every kiss, every tender touch, even the hot breath of passion
is a blessing that gods, if they lived, would envy us. Loving
etches names and faces into memories that last long after
their bearers have moved on to other vows, other embraces,
or have left this troubled realm of struggling for better or worse.
Where are all those whom I have loved and who left me
a swish and shock of hair, the soft seashell of an ear,
the moist allure on a pair of lips, a nutbrown nipple erect
in the palm? Are any of them searching for my name and face
in the scrub and spinney of passion among tokens of spent love?
Threescore and ten, and still learning
That life is the balance it maintains,
Still learning that our losses
Are the measure of our gains.

In the clock's hands the happiest hours dissolve in tears,
yet if there were no love and loving we would turn to stone.
Hand in hand lovers walk across their solitude into forgetting
or they lean over the parapet to watch the swirling waters
of a stream or river pass under the bridge, their arms tight
around each other's mortality. At night they lie in a bed
glittering with stars, wondering why and how to close the gap
between what they know and what they understand, embracing
between what they desire and what they attain moments of ecstasy
as their yearnings pass through the stricture of love's hourglass.
Threescore and ten, and still learning
To divest myself of certainties,
Still learning to seize the moment
And let go of the mind's eternities.

One by one and year by year friends and lovers depart, often
without farewells, ghosts melting into that night without future.
What remains are shivers of what they were, beloved shades
at the mercy of my memory, as I shall be at yours, programmed
in the convoluted brain to repeat the foolish and the fair,
the thoughtless and the loving, the crooked and the kind acts
stored in the hard drive of our hearts until we can no longer
call them up, one by one they vanish in the darkness and silence
from which birth fetched us for this loud and luminous interlude.
The fires of friendship go out and leave us shivering in our solitude.
Threescore and ten, and still learning
That joy is the other half of pain,
Still learning that just being here
Is triumph enough over the inane.

Yet shades and shadows authenticate light; the darker they are
the more brilliant the light they move across. If all were light
we would live in darkness. Moving between the two is life—
a zone insensible to grand words and gestures, but illumined
by the robin's liquid song at dawn, the ululant cry of the loon
at dusk, the delirium of a rose garden in July, the sweet tart bite
of an October apple, a breath of morning air, sunshine, a glass
of wine, a handshake, rain, a log crackling in the fireplace
while it snows outside, a lover's hand touching, brushing
the skin gently, a friend's word, a loving word—that's all I ask.
Threescore and ten, and still learning
That fragile nature has it over ageless art,
Still learning it is the simple things
That cheer and nourish the human heart.

It's in Your Bones
(on his 75th birthday)

It's in your bones that you begin to sense
a change of season: winter is acomin' —
one by one the birds fall silent, you hear
the wind down from the north whistling
through its icicle teeth, calling you back.

It's in your bones you feel the years pull
you up a path which holds no promise
of a mountain peak, steeper and steeper
the daily climb above your memories
which lead back down the way you came.

It's in your bones you first experience
the pangs of slack flesh and stiff joints
as appetites assume absurd proportions
launching hot-air balloons of desire
the tiny pricks of age puncture and deflate.

It's in your bones you come to know the folly
of generations generating more generations
all for a quick tumble in the fatal sun
their bones alone outlasting them a little
way into the tunnel that ends in the dark.

And yet there is in these bones the marrow
of yet another tomorrow where love roots
deeper in the furious flesh and the sun spins
earth forever round and round the seasons
forcing flower and song from the sullen void.

Part of it is a bone of contention that rises
in the court of love to argue on the evidence
the case for ecstasy quite literally to stand above
the dying flesh defiant of inevitable defeat
triumphant in the final, unfair judgment of time.

It's in your bones — that ecstasy of the green
blood singing in trees and grasses, and the red
river running through your heart to blossom
into a mind where the world grows young again
every time you open your eyes to know you are
here still, still strutting your piece to the sky,
still wondering and trying to figure out why.

Dialogue with a Polish Poet

(for Wistawa Szymborska)

1. A Final Exam

I too dream of a final exam
on the history of human kind
but it's a nightmare
Brueghel never painted:
the two monkeys are invigilators,
they hand me the exam paper,
there's nothing written on it—
just drawings: three mounds
of shoes
        —as in Auschwitz
of skulls
        —as in Cambodia
of ashes
        —as in Hiroshima.

It's a multiple choice exam
but I don't know the question
and the monkeys won't tell me:
one of them is masturbating
while the other is picking his fleas.

I wake in a sweat
between simians and semiotics.

2. A Matter of Language

"Vous habitez au Canada?" he exclaimed. "C'est comme exister dans un frigidaire, n'est-ce pas?" He had never visited Canada. Or any other country. What for? France had everything he needed. And you could travel the rest of the world more comfortably on TV.

"Monsieur," I felt like saying, "our poets write with icicles in the snow. The arctic wind blows their words away, and images freeze to their skin. That's why no one has ever heard of them. It's different with our women. They're famous for the fur coats, fur boots, fur hats and the nosebags they wear. Except in bed, mostly. Of course none of us Canadians ever wears boots without skis or skates attached to them. Except in bed. Really, sir."

I had it on my tongue to say all that, but my tongue was frozen. You see, I don't know the language well enough.

"Le Canada? C'est comme exister dans un frigidaire, n'est-ce pas?"

"Oui, monsieur," I replied. "Comme en France on habite dans un baril de vin."

3. An Even Larger Number

Seven billion people on earth
and my imagination is changing.
It multiplies by two thousand
the planet's population at the time
the neolithic revolution changed everything,
and watches the transformation
of forests into fields, fields into deserts.
It conjures crystal-clear rivers and lakes
turning toxic as a thinning sky
renders the life-giving sun lethal.

And I multiply by a few generations
a billion faces of endurance and suffering,
each with a name, a mother, a memory—
and watch them spread in a black rain
like a carpet of dying flowers
across every continent.

Perhaps Dante didn't get it right
because he watched the Black Death
carry off two thirds of Europe's people
and he couldn't read the signs
because the politics of Guelphs and Ghibellines
obscured nature's adroit balancing-act.

As for what lives after us
it's all a matter of time.
Fame too dies, as surely as planets do.
Horace got it right: *ars longa,*
vita brevis est, or as Chaucer put it:
the lif so short, the craft so long to lerne.
To be alive can never be enough for us
but it's all we've got, and
we have it to make choices
and in choosing we affirm what we deny.

A poem at the price of a life.
So many die whom we could save
while I write and you read a poem.
A witness is always an accomplice,
but if we don't fit words to the occasion
the world will never be entirely alive.
Poems don't move mountains
but a sigh is better than a shrug.

My dreams aren't all nightmares.
I remember them in my poems—
those solitudes I share
with friends dead and alive,
those spaces I outgrow
as I learn to occupy them.

Sometimes the imagination opens a door
behind which an infinite space
full of stars and voices is waiting
and you know that if
you ever cross its threshold
you will fall and fall
forever.

Sailing the Seven C's

It took a few thousand
million years to write
the chronicle of life
with only four letters
to the alphabet of transmission
winding and unwinding a stairway
spiralling up and down to the stars.

Moving forward, microbes
discovered two are better
than one, three better still
and so forth—so long
as each plays and perfects
a different part in the all-out
prizefight for survival.

It took a few thousand
million years for three to reach
beyond their blind grasp
and breed a hundred trillion,
learning in the process that
in time cooperation beats
aggression claws down.

A hundred trillion joined
forces in a cooperative
search for the carbon
route across the palpable
darkness on the seven seas
to reach shore past countless
dead ends in glorious light.

It took a hundred trillion
microbes to build
the wand'ring bark
to sail the open waters
between drifting continents:
our gilled foremothers knew
their way about the oceans.

We are on a journey
across vast expanding
spaces spinning the secret
that compels mind to emerge
from chaos and deliver us
to an uncertain future
in the dawn of consciousness.

Guided by communication
among vital cells
a hundred billion neurons play
a game of chance in the dark
involutions under the skull
betting on our creativity
to comprehend the incomprehensible.

It takes a hundred billion
neurons to nurture
in the limbic system compassion
for the living coded
to yearn for immortality
knowing they are on the path
to everlasting oblivion.

Is this a numbers game
only? How much further
do we have to travel
tempestuous complexities
before mind stretches
the eternities of mathematics
to include our dreams?

The music of the spheres
will embrace everything
in the final realization
that nothing has ever been
anything but mind
inflating the many dimensions
of a black hole

launching a cooperative
of microbes on its passage
from chaos through complexity
via communication and creativity
to the emergence
of comprehension
and compassion.

Caravaggio

(Exhibition at the National Gallery, Ottawa, summer 2011)

No Angelo this Michel:
short and hot tempered
he quarrelled with the world
of bankers, cardsharks and cardinals
forcing them into the light
to play their part unmasked
in the age-old human comedy.

He met humanity's mountebanks
in the vicolos and trattorias of Rome
and walked them sacred and profane
in their everyday skins and clothes
straight onto his canvases
to crowd out the darkness
with their crooked love of life:

fortune-telling gypsies pick-pocketing
as their own pockets are picked,
nubile musicians performing
madrigals lamenting a lover's loss,
god-fearing saints enduring
their sufferings like good sinners,
and bawds embodying holy virgins.

They beckon us to join them
in a flurry of hands—hands soft,
hard-bitten, nimble, callous, nervy.
With fingers graceful as spiders' legs
or solid as sausages, hands that know
to pluck the lute's and the heart's strings
and to drive plough and sword home.

An orgy of touching and feeling
chiaroscuro captured in colour.
He looked in the mirror and saw
Bacchus, his fragile flesh yearning
for a brush with danger, saw
that no prison could hold or cure
him from the fever that is life.

Self-portrait
(Van Gogh, Saint-Rémy, 1889)

Cadmium yellow
the light rises
from the palette's
fire: the artist
thrusts his hand
into it holds it there
without flinching
endures the flame
struggling up under
bold brute strokes
in blue to surge
lambent between green
cascading shadows and
ignite across his face
a flare in the vertiginous dark.

Here I am
for want of a model
you are there
for want of a mirror.

I return from the violet reeling
madness of your world
filled with the demons
of poverty and disease
—then as now.
In August I had another brush
with death, the almost smiling
little reaper
under the big sun
scything flesh
as though it were wheat.
But for you, my brother
I'd be there already under
the mauve-tainted brown earth
with one painting sold for a pittance.

Between the bloodline of the lip
and the gold flickering in his hair
the exacting eyes implacable
centre of all movement and colour
staring inward and outward seeing
between the iron bars
of a cell a dark horse
and a ploughman in the stubble
a wheatfield with cypresses
sold a century later
to an American tycoon
for $57 million.

Here I saw that
far ahead
the madness
was there already.

I have only 5 francs left,
my dear Theo, so I must beg
you send me paints brushes
and 10 meters of canvas I don't want
to fall into the hands of
the police and get carried off
to an asylum by force I haven't left
my room in two months eating
only bread and a little soup
I'm working from morning to night
like a miner who is always in
danger I think this will help
cure me for a new attack
is due probably three months
from now in winter before my easel
I feel somewhat alive.

Dark the circles menacing
violet-blue like a halo
of death the head
is a torch. Something is burning
behind the viridian ghost skin
barely holding back the pain
stretched tight across rugged brows
down hollow orange-stubbled cheeks.
His eyes stare translucent
from a skull full of sunflowers,
star-crazed nights, flaming cypresses,
the portraits of peasants, doctors
and of countless manic selves
in an austere bedroom they pierce
centuries and tycoons, transfix them
forever with a stroke of his sullen
brush spinning visions.

There are beautiful things to be done:
the vineyards and the olive orchards—
silver against a soil of orange
and violet hues under a large white
sun my mind is absolutely
wandering between the mirror
and the model it is
with people as with wheat
in the end we are ground
between millstones
to become bread.

Celebration in November

(for Arlette)

Mist rises grey from the leaf-composting ground,
climbs barren branches to shroud the trees
and smears a leaden light across the sky.
November is not a month to pick flowers.
The ashen face of its days refuses to smile
whatever cause for celebration we conjure
and its damp nights make gooseflesh even
of the limbs of lovers entangled in their desires.

The rain too is grey and steady, runs to melancholy
seeping dripping rolling down roofs trees walls
and windows as though day and night determined
to dissolve in tears, or melt away in shadows
to escape the icy claws of winter poised to strike
and tear the subdued light briskly into blizzards.

Yet in the landscape of my heart there is a valley
where flowers blossom at the touch of love
at any season, where clean streams wash away
the day's warts and worries and at night the sun
is a golden avalanche in the thighs of mountains.
It's not a dream that you and love were born
in November for dreamers hug but empty air:
I hold in my arms the fullness of two lives paired.

In this valley of my heart I'll always celebrate
what's improbable — the chance that brought us here,
the light that from the beginning implied us
as the rose implies its colour and its fragrance,
and our love that's granted us time out from drudgery
and dying, absurdly glorious, for a song and a dance.

Inscrutable November that under its damp grey cloak
concedes such celebrations of flesh and flowers
as to confound us and the law of thermodynamics.

Amaryllis

Sirens scream at the drowsy city
as an ambulance chases a silent stalker
that lies in ambush in the dark passageways
connecting the body's many dwellings
to the extremities of the heart.

A victim choking in the killer's hold
is snatched from certain death at zero hour
and delivered to emergency. The attack
is registered, compressed into dates and data,
the patient poked, probed and injected.

The stalker refuses to surrender
his vital statistics, but medication
puts him in his place, and his intended victim
takes heart as he is wheeled to a ward
for the surgeon's inquest and sentence.

The long dark tunnel from emergency
is chilly and foreboding. Fear creeps
into the mind's folds. The heart, worn
from the burdens of living, falters:
will it rally to beat the odds in the morning?

Tracks crisscross the ceiling of each ward
to run curtains round the solitude
of those in pain. Little of what is left
of their pride huddles in hives of hope
where tiny flames strobe-light the will to live.

Patients pushed and pulled in wheelchairs
or on hospital gurneys between labs, surgery
and their cubicles, mostly men, mostly old,
semi-private, semi-conscious, semi-alive
and semi-dead, their manhood diminished

till even their patience goes limp. And I
grow weary of waiting among the promises
of well-meaning doctors and the solicitations
of smiling nurses. I know the killer bides his time
in the blood and the heart cannot be institutionalized.

Dawn presses a grey blanket damp against the window.
I hear the winter wind whistle a dirge in the streets below,
blowing flurries of snow horizontally across the cold light.
Five storeys above the just awakening Ottawa traffic
I feel my years like a heavy weight in my flesh and bones.

And there, at the centre of my anxiety,
between drab hospital walls and insipid meals,
an explosion of blood-red petals—an amaryllis!
Nine blossoms succulent as passion, a gift of love
feeding the flames in one of my nine lives.

Buds rose on sturdy green legs hour by hour
from the first day of my confinement
unfolded till they towered above the ailing
wannabe living forever and a day—
a cluster of floral flesh and blood

like a circle of dancers suspended in mid-air,
mouths wide open, all lips and loving,
anthers tonguing the clinical air,
their crimson petals velvet skirts flaring—
a tableau to trump mortality for another day.

The sirens were silent when I went home,
the blood once more coursing freely
through the re-enforced tunnels in the flesh,
an amaryllis singing a Renaissance glee
to the tune of a newly enchanted heart.

Post Mortem Anniversary

So a decade has passed, father,
since you fell silent and returned
to the dark earth, leaving all that music
you conjured from the piano
to play in my memory over and over
to a slow fade. I can hear you now
only when the hour reaches its still point.
(They say you can't take it with you,
but you did: you took what was you
and disappeared into the night.)

You never were much of a talker.
Our arguments about Marx, jazz,
women (did we ever talk of women?),
god and Nietzsche—what mattered
was always left unsaid. You preferred
to talk with your fingers: the keys
on the grand piano unlocked you.
(And you were absolutely right:
the winds of change tear everything
we cherish to shreds, even truth.)

Your admonitions and reprimands,
scoldings and prohibitions—did they
point me in the right direction? Did they
test my mettle as I navigated my fate
like a somnambulist? You meant well
but your own embattled ship foundered
in the dark turbulence of the times.
(And I? Oh the many scenarios
I could write for other, better lives
that might have been me!)

It's what we didn't talk about
that I remember best: where a look
into the pit was all we dared
and we pretended not to see
the pool of tears at the bottom
and in each other's eyes.
(We looked the other way
and left it all to music
so fragile were we at the core
a word could have broken us.)
So we used words sparingly,
sparing our emotions and affections,
thin words cut into my memory
like lines for an ink drawing of you,
of us, of all those troubled years
we never said we loved each other.
We wanted to but did not know how.
(Had we not learnt to trust the world
that language left us so naked we hid
in the furthest corners of silence?)

I search my memory for your face
and find a pained, tormented look
the day war burst into our lives
like shrapnel. You were not born
to be a soldier, nor I born to serve
a lunatic, but we remained silent.
(Why did we never talk about what
I could never stop thinking of—
the pain, the shame, the horror?
What if I had asked the right question?)

Some day my children too will search
their memories for me and wonder
what they might have said or done
or asked, and why they didn't, as I wonder
today when you would have been ninety.
I am closer to you now that you are gone
into the night that answers no questions.
(I shall never know where you came from
or who you were. Our memory is a trailer
from a movie that cannot be rerun.)

Only the music lingers, the melodies,
the rhythms, and the intimacies between them
sing out what we could never put into words.

Requiem for a Sicilian Artist

(for Rito Caltabiano in memoriam)

His was a sturdy race of islanders
tempered in the kiln of sun and rock.
No Greek or Arab, Roman or Phoenician
could bend to their swords a people who learnt
to draw oil and wine from streams of lava.

An ancient volcano rocked his cradle;
its fountains of fire and ash ignited
in his eye a flame that taught his hand
to reach beyond the burning river
before it consumed his heart.

And he learnt to draw the face of Sicily
into landscapes where the Ionian light leaps
across palm trees and red-tiled roofs to dance
on the boisterous sea through fishermen's nets
into the eyes of peasants haggard as the soil.

But stone feeds no mouths and the sun burns up
more than it fuels. So he left what might have been
and took his brush and his dreams north northwest
across an ocean to a faraway half-frozen land
more alien than the moon over Mount Etna.

Here winter and the icy rules of engagement
chilled his spirit and darkness fell in his heart.
Like a blind man he tapped a painted cane
to find his way, but in a world of bilk and money
art must wait on the whims of fools.

Perhaps sometime in the middle of a winter night
with a howling wind honing icicles on eaves
something delicate broke inside him, something
not for sale in the flea market of impostors,
something irreparable that rendered his sun black.

The gold he sought was hidden in the light;
when it went out he packed away his brush
and his palette, wrapped them in his tattered dreams
and in the stillness stole away to return home
to the sun-hewn island of his first and final sleep.

The Jade Canoe
(Bill Reid's sculpture)

Sculpted in clay and cast in bronze this canoe
is launched on troubled seas crammed with dreams
that surf and break against the rock coast of dawn,
a casual crew paddling in no manifest direction.

The bear in the lookout bow has turned his back
to the wind. Nor can the raven at the helm see
past the inscrutable skipper what's coming and to come.
The mouse woman is in the dark, too timid to paddle.

Is this a native ark packed with the remains
of fish, flesh and fowl after the final tsunami,
paddling a wave of hope to find everlasting land
and start once more the story of living and dying?

Or is it a leaky life-boat running from the storm
that sank their ship, its survivors paddling fear
to reach *terra firma* in a magic circle drawn
about them by the ever receding horizons?

At the centre of the journey, above the frenzy
of escape and search, a man/woman tower commands
the erratic crew to thrust their oars in the void
and paddle beyond understanding to calmer seas.

Ship of fools. The eagle cannot take flight
when the wolf sinks its voracious teeth in its wings.
Nor can the beaver's eager oar paddle the canoe
to any destination other than a stagnant pool.

A dead fish hoisted on a harpoon points to the future
while somewhere, bleached and weathered, Haida totems
crosshatch the sky. The jade canoe must paddle on and
carry passengers and crew to shelter in uncertain ports.

Indifferent to the difference between land and sea
the smug frog dozes in the shadow of the eagle's
foolish assault on the bear. Only the dogfish woman
sees past her hooked nose the hidden coast approach.

She's not fooled by the green patina. She knows
this tableau is not carved in stone, knows the raven
steers and they all paddle a cargo of living myths
and dying memories everywhere and nowhere.

Starry Nights

1. Arles, 1888

Stars blossom like spring flowers
amidst a sprinkling of pink and green
in the night's cobalt blue fields
where a dream as majestic as the galaxies
paints frescoes across the darkness
the Great Bear inhabits so brilliantly.
From his jet blue lair he gazes
on the ruthless town trying to set fire
to the river, throwing its gas lights
on the languid blue black waters
that cannot put them out
or carry them off downstream.
Blue here is not a mood
but a celebration and a ritual
as it bleeds from blackness into light—
Vincent's vision of the Rhône
and the universe!

The river fractures
the half asleep town and juggles
the pieces red gold and bronzed green
all night long to put them together
again. But relentless the currents
bend and stretch the reflections
and muttering in indigo they eddy
toward the faraway mediterranean-blue sea.

How yellow must have been his house
that so much blue should make a river
and a night the afterimage in his inward eye!
He was waiting for a friend's passion
to help him endure the grandeur and the terror
of such vast blue glittering darkness that dwarfs
the couple out for a stroll among the stars.
Arm in arm they've turned their backs
on the river for they've come to terms
with time lapping softly at its banks
as they walk the blue green path in a dream
of love they share with the painter
under the cold cobalt sky and his brush.

2. Åsgårdstrand, 1893

Even the light is nothing but pools of blue
shadows washing against darker shapes
in a landscape midway between the garden
of the gods and the mind's forlorn eye
looking as through a blue glass. Everything
suggests what is invisible. Night is brooding
over the enigma of its dreams. The sun
ambiguously smears and smudges the cobalt
sky across infinity—bitter blue
scrim wrinkled above a smoother sea
lapping north into purple. Where they meet
a scar alludes to an ancient wound.
A pale fence cuts sharply into Ymir's flesh
and points to the ocean filled with his sweat
and blood. From his brain they made the murky
clouds and from his brow the enclosed
garden that harbours the night's dark
longing. Summer is here a short blue
black fire that has fused three linden
trees into a fist raised to defy dawn.
Or is it a skull rising from long interment
deep in the earth still half buried with its secrets
kept below ground by the dreaded darkness?
The moon's sickle splits the domed shadow
midway between blind ocular pits. A faint
reddish form hints at what might be
a hut in or beyond the trees in or beyond
a legend perhaps of Ask and Embla to whom love
was born of mystery and longing in the twilight
of unrecorded time.

Many blues compose
the vast sadness of this universe
where a pair of lovers is pinned naked
against the slatted fence embracing
their shadows that we may not know
their final illicit consummation.
This sombre midgard is no place
for immortals. Venus peers vacant across
the desolate horizon at the stars
in the constellation of Aries stretched out
in the blueing waters that stroke the land
in its sleep. Tranquillity is painted here:
a dark mask behind which myth
and menace move shadows
in charcoal blue to melancholy.

3. Ayorama, 1997

On a clear night the cosmos blows its cold breath
into my face as I search for patterns
in the speckled heavens a mad pointillist
might have painted in silver on aubergine
black canvas stretched from horizon to horizon.

Orion rests one foot on the cedar-shingled roof
his sword dangling nebulously from his belt
to create the impression of a Greek god
in pursuit of beauty: Andromeda riding
Pegasus off the edge of the western world.

Night is the master of illusions, conjuring
in a blue black haze gods that are but passing
configurations of stars and galaxies strung together
by sightlines cross-hatching images lifted
from dreams. If you refuse to be deceived
you're left with black holes devouring light
as irretrievably as whales sweep up diatoms,
or superstrings that tie the galaxies in knots
with threads as invisible as those the daughters
of the night spin to weave our fate. The sky
speaks in paradigms. You cannot know
what you know in this world of whirling
worlds where a thimbleful of matter can weigh
more than the moon, and some objects shine
brighter than a trillion suns.

                                 Tonight the stars
are sizzling in the sky, their fires cold as space
and I revel in the irrelevancy of being
here and now, listening to the light buzz
like myriads of stellar flying bugs. Tinier
than an atom in a grain of sand I stand
on a speck of dust lost in many dimensions
and yet I can embrace the universe that knows me
not. The bull's eye of Aldebaran is blind
but I can see the Pleiades overhead give birth
to new stars and parade their blue giants
on the Milky Way. Something inside me unfolds
wings angels would envy me for they carry me
through nebulae and supernovae from quarks
to quasars in an ever expanding universe
beyond the borders of spacetime even
as my own clock winds down the shrinking years.

The night is full of memories of the many worlds
we inhabit: the tranquillity of stars and their terror;
the distances that temper their blazing fury
which gives us life; and the lightning speed
at which we careen ceaselessly with them
through interstellar voids. From the unfathomable
dark above us to the ultramarine grey stillness
through which trees filter all impressions, peace
flows and fills our hearts though we know nothing
stands still. All is motion and motion is all
evolution. We're spinning in all directions
as we stand still, evolving in the very act
of looking at the glittering circles of this sky.

Hold me, love, hold me in a tight embrace
that we may know we are not alone
in this thundering silence. We are such stuff
as stars are made of and must share,
for better and for worse, their fate. Let us, love,
be their most exquisite consummation.

Notes

"**Ayorama**" is the name I gave to the loghouse I built on 100 acres of woodland near Maxville, Ontario. My partner, Arlette Francière, and I lived there for over three decades, raised our daughter Clara there, and pursued our creative commitments. The pond, big enough for a canoe and a rowboat, I excavated in the middle of the bush, prompted a visiting Chinese scholar to declare that we lived *life by a Canadian Walden Pond.* — "Ayorama" is an Inuit word which I translate as "it's destiny".

"**Mer Bleue**" is a 3,500-acre conservation area on the eastern outskirts of Ottawa. It is perhaps the most remarkable part of the city's Green-belt. With its 7,700-year-old bog, the area offers a flora and fauna more typical of northern boreal wetlands than the Ottawa valley.

"**El Mirbed**" is the name of a pan-Arabic poetry festival held annually in Baghdad. I was told it dates back to the Middle Ages. The name means "the place where the camel squats down," i.e. in the evening when the caravan comes to rest for the night by an oasis after a hot day in the desert sun. That's the time for the storytellers to regale and relax the tired travellers. I was fortunate enough to be one of a hand-ful of poets from outside the Arabic world to be invited to participate in this international festival. I attended for four consecutive years in the eighties, and I can testify to the enthusiasm with which audiences flocked by the hundreds and thousands to these poetry recitals — at least until the USA brutally destroyed civilized life in Iraq.

The "Manifesto in Times of War" was my answer to a poem by a princess-poet from Kuwait who rhapsodized the war effort (against Iran) at the El-Mirbed Festival in Baghdad (1986), declaring that this was no time for poetry and that she'd trade a hundred poets for one soldier. I wrote the poem in anger overnight, and it was read the next day in English and in Arabic — to the consternation of the many army officers in the large audience.

"Letter to the Goddess of Flowers" was written after viewing the Indian film, *Bandit Queen* (1994), based on the extraordinary life of Phoolan Devi (Seema Biswas) who suffered the abuse and indignities of a member of a lower caste as a child. It turned her into a revengeful criminal and finally into a combative politician, a story both tragic and heroic.

The "Jade Canoe" won first prize in poetry at the Surrey International Writers' Conference in Vancouver in 2006.

Acknowledgements

Some of the poems in this collection have been published in various magazines, such as *Anthos, Ariel, The Canadian Forum, Decabration, Corridors, Fiddlehead, The Harpweaver, Humanist Perspectives, Poetry Canada,* and *Verse Afire.* I thank the editors for their trust in my work.

My special and warmest thanks go to my wife and partner, Arlette Francière, not only for her passionate love of poetry, but also for the tireless practical help in assembling this collection, her sensitive and intelligent response to the individual poems, and for her impeccable proofreading. She is a splendid artist in her own right, both as painter and as translator, and I deeply appreciate her sharing her formidable gifts and her generous spirit with me.

Poetry Collections by Henry Beissel

WITNESS THE HEART (1963)

NEW WINGS FOR ICARUS (1966)

THE WORLD IS A RAINBOW (1968)

THE PRICE OF MORNING (transl. Walter Bauer, 1968)

FACE ON THE DARK (1970)

THE SALT I TASTE (1975)

A DIFFERENT SUN (transl. Walter Bauer, 1976)

CANTOS NORTH (1980, 1982)

SEASON OF BLOOD (1984)

POEMS NEW AND SELECTED (1987)

AMMONITE (1987)

A THISTLE IN HIS MOUTH (transl. Peter Huchel, 1987)

STONES TO HARVEST (1987, 1993)

DYING I WAS BORN (1992)

LETTERS ON BIRCHBARK (transl. Uta Regoli, 2000)

THE DRAGON & THE PEARL (2002)

ACROSS THE SUN'S WARP (2003)

THE METEOROLOGY OF LOVE (2010)

COMING TO TERMS WITH A CHILD (2011)

SEASONS OF BLOOD (2012)

FUGITIVE HORIZONS (2013)

COMING TO TERMS WITH A CHILD / EIN KIND KOMMT ZUR
    SPRACHE (bilingual edition, 2015)

FUGITIVE HORIZONS / FLÜCHTIGE HORIZONTE (bilingual
    edition, German translation by Heide Fruth-Sachs, 2015)

About The Author

Henry Beissel was born in Cologne (Germany). His father was a pianist whose career was cut short when the Nazis came to power. By temperament and disposition an outsider, he is subjected as a child to the ubiquitous regimentation of dictatorship and develops a vehement and permanent hatred for authority. His youth is shattered in air raids and bomb shelters in what he regards as one of the cruellest wars in history because much of it was directed against unarmed women and children. A voracious reader, he finds in books the only sane and rational world he has ever known. He begins to write before the age of ten as a clandestine way of asserting his freedom.

The end of the war is traumatic because it brings revelations of Nazi atrocities that fill him with horror and shame which eventually drive him out of Germany in 1949 to go and continue his studies in philosophy at the University of London. It took him almost 70 years to deal with his childhood trauma in a cycle of autobiographical poems, *Coming to Terms with a Child* (Black Moss, 2011), which has been republished with his own German version, *Ein Kind kommt zur Sprache* (Verlag LiteraturWissenschaft, Marburg, 2015)

Determined to start a new life away from the burdens of the past, he emigrates to Canada in 1951. Years of struggle follow to find himself and to survive economically in Toronto where he held many different jobs from clerking at Canadian Tire to freelancing for CBC radio and television. He writes consistently throughout these years, mainly poetry, and discovers his vocation as a writer. In 1956, he enters the University of Toronto to study English literature to find roots in a new culture, and completes his M.A. in 1960. By now an academic career seems the only possible compromise between his need to support a family and his commitment to serious writing. University posts include Edmonton (1962-64), Trinidad (1964-66) and finally Montreal where he is Professor of English at Concordia University, teaching Literature and Creative Writing for 30 years. In 1996 he retires as Distinguished Professor Emeritus.

His commitment to writing comes to national attention in 1963 when he founds and edits *Edge*, the controversial Journal of the Arts, Literature and Politics. Since then he has written and published extensively—poetry, drama, fiction and non-fiction—over thirty books in all; the most recent is a collection of poetry, *Fugitive Horizons* (Guernica Editions, 2013), a journey across the known and unknown micro- and macrocosm.

Throughout his career as a writer, he is active in all the writers' associations: the Guild of Canadian Playwrights (a co-founder), the League of Canadian poets (president in 1980), and the Writers' Union of Canada (which he represents for a time internationally). He is the recipient of many awards and prizes, including a Senior Canada Council grant, the 1994 Walter Bauer Literary Award, and the Naji Naaman Literary Prize, 2008, Maison pour la culture, Beirut (Lebanon) for his book length poem, "Where Shall the Birds Fly?" In October 2015, the University of Marburg made Beissel an Honorary Member of the Marburg Centre for Canadian Studies "in recognition of his exemplary work representing Canadian literature and culture in Germany."

He has three children, all grown up, and one grandson. He is married to Arlette Francière, painter and distinguished translator (Robertson Davies and W.O. Mitchell into French and Michel Beaulieu into English). She has provided cover artwork for many of his books. Henry and Arlette now live in Ottawa.

Printed in March 2016
by Gauvin Press,
Gatineau, Québec